HUMILIATIONS AND INSPIRATION

An Incomplete Journey of My Life

Hiranya Borah

First Published in April 2022

ISBN: 978-93-5611-399-2

BLUEROSE PUBLISHERS
www.BlueRoseONE.com
info@bluerosepublishers.com
+91 8882 898 898

Cover Design:
Geetkika Kandari

Typographic Design:
Namrata Saini

Distributed by: BlueRose, Amazon, Flipkart

Dedication

Almost sixty years ago, a boy of age two and a half was thrashed black and blue by his father in front of his mother; but his mother did not rescue him from his angry father's wrath for the next few minutes. Finally, the boy picked up firewood and hit his father on his leg with all his might. With an agonising pain, the father left the scene, but the child's mother advised her son not to hit anyone who is older than him in the future without showing any sympathy for the boy. That boy became a self-sufficient 'adult man' from the early age of four and learned everything to survive in this world and promised his mother by the age of five, not to hurt anyone physically who is older than him. Though in the eyes of others he became a successful man in due course of time, he remained an unhappy man because except the Mother Goddess he had never found anyone whenever he was in trouble or was humiliated by someone in his entire life.

It is a story of a doctor friend of mine. However, I am sure his journey of life is not a 'one in a crore case' , and therefore, the book is dedicated to all the people who became successful despite being humiliated at different times, in different situations, and at different places by different persons.

Author

Inspiration

I am extremely inspired by the kind words on my literary works by none other than the Hon'ble Prime Minister of India, Shri Narendra Damodardas Modi on 16th March 2021 at his chamber in the Parliament House when I got my 'one in lifetime' opportunity to handover a copy of my book, Chandrapraha: The Iron Lady of Assam.

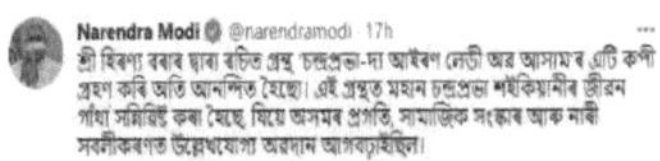

An Admission

Many readers asked me if my earlier novel 'Blessed One' is my autobiography. I always say that it was not. Despite that, the protagonist Kanak Barua's life and my life may have many similarities which many of my known persons also may have discovered while going through the novel. To prove my point, I decided to write my autobiography for my esteemed readers; with few twists and turns.

Though it is my autobiography, I am changing the names of the persons who had humiliated me at different points of time to show my respect for their privacy as they might not know that they had hurt me with their words or through their actions on those occasions. Even I may be a culprit of humiliating others through my actions, though I always try to be nice to others consciously. The people, who had humiliated me, might be nice to others and therefore, it is my perception that they had humiliated me from time to time intentionally. However, I am always thankful to them, because of them I became a tough and tougher guy in my life due to their behaviour towards me.

Further, I am assuring you that all the incidents narrated by me in this book had actually been taken place in my life; however, it's from my own perspective only.

Even when I had only less than one year in service, and many people had often asked me, 'When I was going to settle down?' and when I used to reply that 'I am yet to decide', most of the people thought that I was lying. Honestly, I was yet to take a decision where I was going to stay, at NCR, at Guwahati, or elsewhere even a few days prior to my retirement.

However, at the very next question, 'what I am going to do after my retirement?' I had a very clear answer. I told them that one thing was sure; I shall have an extended fighting time with my lovely wife of more than three and a half decades. No, I am not going to do any statistical works for the Government or against the Government. I shall try to avoid going to any Government office where I had worked in any time during my service life even for few months.

I shall try, to be busy with my first love, writing and composing poetry (I am told by many including my wife that I am lousy in doing so) after my retirement. Another question I have to face a number of times from my Assamese friends, is why I do not write a book in Assamese now. To be frank, I told my sister to publish the Assamese version of my historical novel on Mula Gabharu: A story of Extreme Valour and Patriotism. She talked with some publishers and one of them showed his interest to publish at the condition that the writer gets some sort of clearance from some Assamese historians. I opted out immediately as I have some angst against the Assamese historians for their collective failure in making our historical heroes and heroines at par even with the national historical icons.

However, recently when the same question had been asked by a budding journalist, I promised him to publish some of my romantic poems (which may be liked by the youngsters and hope some of them will be used by some teenagers to propose to their crushes. I am sure, some of my senior friends will laugh while reading those poems and I expect some of them may even condemn the poems. I promise all of you, the publication will be world class in terms of visual presentation even if the poems may be of 'third-class quality' in your eyes.

Making of a trilingual film on Mula Gabharu in my mind is always disturbing me like the rejection of my love proposals by many beautiful ladies in my entire life due to poor background, rustic behaviour, age and so on. But I am always hopeful; like agreeing to marry me by my wife committing a Himalayan Blunder, there will be a way out to make the trilingual film now.

There is an old saying, 'a single photograph can explain 1000 relations. Following that old saying, I have given few photographs of some of my near and dear ones under the title 'Photo Album'. I have not written much in the book about my relation and closeness with the photographed persons. Readers may infer my relation with the persons from the caption under each photograph. However, I have also given some scope for speculations as well.

Preface

On 13 February, 1992, I met Mother Goddess in my dream. She advised me to discard my most favorite items of food and food products; meat and meat products for having a long and successful life of my elder daughter. Therefore, I left meat and meat products including chicken etc. since 14.02.1992 coinciding with Valentine's Day.

Again, the Mother Goddess came in my dream, a few years ago and asked me to make a choice between two different types of life of mine. The first choice was simple, 'you die early with a peaceful life, but the members of your family have to struggle in their life.'

The second option given to me was, 'you will have a horrible, humiliating long life; but the other members of your family will have a comfortable and secure long life. Further, if you opt for the second option, all in this world including your own family members will forget your good works for their welfare, your help, and sacrifice for your nuclear and extended family, and none will be grateful to you. Not only that, you have to die all alone at a secluded place and before your death, wild animals will eat up some portion of your body. Your misery will not stop there, since your rituals will not be done by any of your family members, your soul will have to roam near your skeleton which will be used by medical students in a medical college. After a few decades, due to an accidental fire, your skeleton will be burnt to ashes. That will be good news for you. From that day onwards, your soul will be able to move around the world; but still, you will not be able to be free from the 'painful life of a soul' till some descendants of your family accidentally visit the holy temple of Dwaraka. Again, there is a catch, if the descendant comes within the seven generations only then you will get the 'moksh (free from all the earthly desires)', otherwise your suffering will continue till the present earth completes her life. In other words, the second option has only one silver lining, your children and wife will have a long, happy, and contented life.'

She stopped there and looked at me for my answer. Without much thought, I opted for the second option.

She told me with a smile, 'it will be like that only, as you have opted for a choice which will give you a life full of pains, heartbreaks, humiliations, unfulfilled desires, and whatnot. But it is your choice; you are responsible for your life.'

She vanished and I got my wits back. I thanked the Mother Goddess for giving me a boon for the happy and long life of my children and my wife.

From that day onwards, I became a happy and an ever-smiling man.

A man is judged for his actions, reactions, good deeds, bad deeds, fulfilling of duties etc., etc. by others. I do not know whether I am a failed son or a successful son for my parents. They are no more to give an answer on this issue today. But whether I am a good relative or a bad relative, I have scores of relatives by blood or through matrimonial alliances who can comment on this issue freely behind me. As a husband, probably I have totally failed just like many other husbands in the world, if I go by the constant accusations hurled on me at least twice in a week by my beloved wife of three and half decades. So is the case, as a father for my three children. Again, as an officer, from my ACRs, it is very clear that I was a very bad officer (average officer; when DPC from Director to the post of DDG was held, the designated board found me unfit for the promotion as some of the ACRs when I was working as Deputy/ Joint Director were only 'Good' which was below the benchmark for the promotion from Director to DDG) for some of my extremely efficient and intelligent senior reporting officers. However, as per the APAR as Director and DDG since 2011, I was an excellent officer in the eyes of my seniors, always having scores of more than 9/10. Since, I am a late bloomer, perhaps my brain, communication skill, etc. developed in the later part of my service career. As a senior officer, I never harmed any of my juniors' careers, so I may not be a very bad officer in the eyes of any of my juniors, though they might be thinking that being an average officer, I found all of them outstanding officers and therefore, I cannot be given any credit for giving them outstanding ACRs and APAR all along with my service career. However, due to my straight talk, I may not be a good officer for both seniors and juniors. Another aspect being a male, readers may be interested to know about my relations with the younger ladies working with me for a few months to a few years in my long service career of more than 36 years and the other ladies who happened to meet me with some social and official works in my last four and a half decades since I gained my adulthood. For 99.99% (one in 10,000) of the young ladies who travelled alone with me thousands of KM, stayed alone with me in a closed room for hours, may give a good certificate on my character as a reliable man who always respects the dignity of a lady. But as you know, even 0.01% is also a very good number in Indian contexts, and therefore, if you luckily meet any of the young ladies coming in the group of 0.01%, you may start hating me as a very bad man towards young ladies. I do not mind that, history is the witness; every alpha man was like that only. Further, this 0.01% does not include even any distant relatives of mine or my wife, wives and children of any of friends and colleagues, any service officers of my service, any subordinates who worked with me for many years, any students whom I taught and who think I was their teacher and any girls whom I address as 'sweetheart', 'sweety', 'darling', 'beta', 'jee', 'bhatijee' 'bhagini' and 'bhanji'. However, I use the word 'darling' to my wife also after a peg or two as exceptional cases. Then who all are left out. The world is too big, you can find many eligible ladies for a night or two if you behave like me. Oh sorry, you are all good people unlike me to have a relation with any lady except your beloved wife. I normally forget the names of my friends who accompanied me where and when therefore those friends of mine should not have a 'cold sweat' who accompanied me to some forbidden places while going through this book.

My greatest failure in life is not able to discard a few 'words of wisdom' in my life which I wanted to discard with all my mental efforts after facing thousands of bad experiences following these lines of my parents as gospel truth. As I was a son of teacher parents, they used to utter these sentences quite frequently, and unfortunately, these sentences had been embedded in my brain which I could not discard despite my lifelong struggle to discard those. When I realized I was a victim of those teachings, it was too late for course correction and all of the family members had already become victims of these erroneous teachings. Now perhaps, even if I am able to discard these 'words of wisdom', there will be no practical value for me at least.

First 'words of wisdom' are 'money is not everything' or 'if money is lost nothing is lost'. Now I do not believe in these two old statements after facing so many bad experiences in my life of six decades due to money crunches. In my life, due to the money crunch, as a student, I could not do many things for my career building. Similarly, I could not provide many facilities to my children which hampered their career progression in the desired fashion. Luckily, as

I did not hanker for a beautiful house and costly furniture, I had never felt any hindrance on that account. However, I could not make happy my wife on that account also.

Second words of wisdom are 'if health is lost, something is lost'. For regaining your health, you need money and that is why we see lots of appeal in the social media for crowd funding. Again, ultimately money plays a pivotal role in regaining lost health. Many people, over emphasize when a rich person dies even after spending a lot of money on some incurable disease, downplaying the fact that thousands times more poor people are dying for not having money to treat the same disease.

Thirdly, the statement, 'if character is lost, everything is lost' is nothing but bull shit, in my opinion after going through the lives of great people including the great kings and emperors from time immemorial. Some hearsay (from reliable sources) on some honourable persons of our time also played its role to disbelieve these 'words of wisdom'. Now, I am damn sure that this particular statement is made to exploit the common mass people, might be by a character-loose person with authority or by a stooge of those kings and emperors who had extremely bad characters. Unfold any history book, you will find almost all the powerful and successful people of the history were having more than one wife, having extra marital relations with at least one beautiful lady, amassed wealth by hook or crook, snatched beautiful daughters and wives of others, killed thousands of people to fulfill the lust of power, lust for women and what not. Can you give me one example, when a king is described as a great one unless he extended his kingdom on the dead bodies of innocent soldiers of either side? So to be a powerful and an extremely successful person you must have a character what was told by Maa Lakshmi to her husband, Vishnu during a discussion which someone had recorded, 'who were the bhakts of whom'. According to that discussion, if someone has an extremely good character, he is likely to enter 'Baikunthdham' after his death. But to be a successful man in this 'world of death', one must be, powerful and *lampat* (character-loose person). Maa Laxmi to prove her point, gave the examples of Ravan and Duryodhan who enjoyed their lives as powerful kings and remained kings till their death. On the other hand, most of the youthful days of Pandavas were in the jungles and lived like paupers. Even after the death of Duryodhan, Yudisthir had to rule a country of widows and orphans only. Even the 'so-called Dharmaraj', in the name of conducting Rajsuya Yagna, he had killed through his powerful brothers, many kings and innocent soldiers of either side. Even Dharmaraj cannot be spared from my criticism as a man of lust for unbound power; because in my opinion character does not mean having relation with more than one lady, but it is a combination of many things; otherwise, a dacoit who might not have an illicit relation with any lady other than his wife has to be certified as a good man. In a nutshell, I have learnt through these books on historical and mythological characters, being loose character itself was the gateway of success; but unfortunately, we were taught otherwise and I am a victim of those teachings. So, the choice is yours; if you want to enjoy your life here (while living) after losing all your morality or there (after your death) living in this world with a high moral character. I am sure; all the hypocrites will jump upon me with all guns blazing alleging that I am misguiding the innocent people to discard the 'words of wisdom' which are the mainstay of Indian society (or main tool to exploit the unsuspecting common people).

Anyway, I am not sure, how many people will read my autobiography and how many people will throw my philosophy to the dustbin after reading the book. Nevertheless, I am trying to convey experiences of my life, my learning of life as honestly as possible to justify my line of thinking in this book.

At present, I am a retired senior Government servant after serving in different Ministry/ Departments little over 36 years 3 months as a Direct Recruit Group-A Officer of the Government of India. My last posting was as a Deputy Director-General in the Department of Drinking Water and Sanitation, Ministry of Jal Shakti. I could not get at least two promotions like my other batchmates as according to my department I was an inefficient and corrupt (though tacitly that was not pronounced by any) officer of my batch. Despite that, I have acquired vivid experiences derived from my official postings across the country, numerous visits across India and outside India as well.

Further, though I am presently living at NCR, Delhi but due to my postings in different parts of the country, some of the postings being in the interior of India, I came across different ethnic personalities, culture and food.

I have so far written 190+ English and one Hindi eBooks besides getting published twelve English and two Assamese books.

Before Joining to Central Government after clearing my UPSC (Union Public Service Commission) examination in my first attempt, I was a lecturer in Cotton College as a regular lecturer selected by APSC (Assam Public Service Commission).

As a student, I used to write articles in some Assamese dailies and during that period of time, two of my novels in Assamese were also published.

I have also edited a few books for the APSC aspirants.

I was the Editor, 'Cottonian' for the 55th issue of 'Cottonian' (1979-80).

One of my stories had been made a serial by Prasar Bharati which was aired by DD Kisan having a viewership of almost a crore. Another story on my mother's life has been made a telefilm by DD, Assam and aired in June, 2021 and few repeat telecast afterwards.

My book on the life of Chandraprabha Saikiani was received by the Hon'ble PM in his chamber located in the Parliament house on 16th March, 2021 and tweeted on the book from his personal tweeter handle.

During my service career, I was inducted in many important committees (orders of some of the committees which are not extremely confidential in nature are in the annexure).

As a failed person, learning from bitter truth, I become a motivational lecturer for the youngsters. I also claim myself as a gender specialist.

In a positive note, I need not have to say that, it is the love of my readers for me which inspires me to write books, one after another, in the last five decades. I am thankful to all the officers and officials of RO Assam and Nagaland with whom I had the opportunity to work as a young officer. I am also thankful to all the officers and officials of MOSPI and DDWS (administration led by Shri Samir Kumar Sinha) including the NIC team. Similarly, I am thankful to all the officers and officials of SSC and DPD, Giridih for their support in my initial years of service. Further, I am thankful to these scribes for their constant support in my literary works, viz. Atanu Saikia, Siddharth Bhattacharyya, Deepak Kumar Chaurasiya, Pranjal Pratim Das, Parto Basak, Sarswat Goswami, Sureman Singh, Dibyajyoti Gogoi, Manissh Kumar Pummy, Ankur Kalita, Manish Shukla, Pradeep Rawat, Rima Sharma, Subhash,

Dinesh Kumar Chauhan, Manas Pratim Sharma and Mukul Talukdar. Though I have not mentioned name of any of my seniors (fearing any omission and commission) who had been always supportive towards my career and my personal life, I shall remain grateful to all of them.

Last, but not the least, I am thankful to all my seniors who vowed to spoil my career and personal life for their own satisfaction, not because they were defending the treasury and other interests of the Government of India. Without their personal and professional dislikes for me, I would not have achieved anything in my life including the achievements as a writer and as a good humanbeing. Their actions had made me a tough warrior in my life. I pray to the Almighty for best of their health and spirit.

However, before reading my whole book, I humbly request you to read the story written in the last chapter of the book.

Author

Table of Content

Chapter I: Introduction

I had been a man who was always envious of everyone who was better than me in any field, till I crossed the age of forty. An unhappy man always pretends to be a happy man and following that rule of law, I also always pretended to be a happy man, and always used to keep a broad smile on my face while meeting anyone known to me. I never tried to be a singer, but I was always envious of the singers for their popularity. So was the case for actors, musicians, painters, sportsmen and politicians. But all this had changed one day when I met a popular actress of yester years who was financially in a dire state. I am told by a friend, who is good in tracking these people for many years because of his professional position, that she had to be a glorified prostitute or a call-girl for the last few years who needs a little bit of cajoling alongwith a few thousand bucks for a night (according to him, she was not adverse for a deal on monthly basis also). As I progressed in the ladder of bureaucracy, I had experienced to meet at least some of those so called successful persons who approached me for some small favours. However, when few years ago, I attended a premier show of an Assamese film alongwith the Honourable Chief Minister of Assam and the Departmental Minister, I was aghast to see that the Director of the film did not even mention the name of a respected actor of Assam, sitting in the audience who happened to be the heartthrob of 1970-80 due to some mega-hit Assamese films. I was waiting till the gentleman introduced the last spot boy of his film to the audience (flaunting all the protocols of the Government in the presence of the Chief Minister and other dignitaries), that the gentleman would thank that particular actor for coming to the premier show despite of his old age. But he preferred to thank all the people on the dais except me, (because perhaps he was not aware that I was representing the Central Ministry who had sanctioned the entire amount for his film). The fundamental of that gentleman was very clear, lick the boots of the officer who had handed over the cheque to him for his film. He was even praising miserly about the contribution of the Honourable CM sir, the Honourable Minister sir and other dignitaries on the dais including the boss of the concerned officer who had handed over the contract to him to make the film. The concerned officer was looking for places to hide himself to avoid any backlash from the seniors including the dignitaries of the dais. When the film started after half an hour, I was privileged to be seated with the Honourable CM sir on one side and the boss of the concerned officer on the other side. As expected, the boss became furious at the quality of the film and apparently CM sir was also unhappy about the quality of the film. All the dignitaries left the hall within half an hour of the start of the film as perhaps no one was enjoying the film. As per my information, till today, no other proposal for a feature film has come to the Ministry from that department since they made that horrible film which perhaps bombed at box office also.

Looking at these people, after attending some of those events as an ordinary or a special invitee over the years, I understood their lives (baring few Amitabhs and Sachins) are more challenging than we common people who are (were) not chased by people for autographs. Once they were out of limelight, they have to face lot of difficulties in social and financial fronts. After realizing their problems and plights, I stopped envying them; rather I have full sympathy for these people (except few of them who could maintain their lavish life style due to proper financial planning or due to success of their children in the same profession or in other professions) who have thousands of fans following from their hey days. During Covid times we have seen how many of the artists from different fields had suffered. Therefore, all of us have to appreciate their challenges in their lives and we should understand the tough life behind the opaque curtains of the glamourous life of the artists.

Please do not think that to demean the artists, I have shared my experiences with the artists over the years; my intention to write these few lines to sensitize the common people about the tough life of our artists after their retirement or semi-retirement of their active lives. I personally think, the pensions given to the artists by the Governments are too meagre to maintain a dignified life by these artists (except few lucky artists as mentioned earlier) after their retirement or semi-retirement of their active lives.

Therefore, now please, please do not doubt my smile as a 'pretentious smile of an unhappy person' rather please take it as a smile of a person with a contended life.

I was born to a teachers' family in Rural Assam. My father was a head Master in a High School and my mother was also a head teacher in an ME school.

Since both of my parents were Head Masters, my mother was Head Mistress of a Government middle school and my father established a High School leaving his government job of a High School teacher, unlike most of the village boys, I did not have the liberty to loiter around the village without any work. Everyone in the locality knew us (my elder brother and me) by face, if not by name and therefore we had very little scope to move around without the knowledge of our parents. Otherwise, I have a very ordinary childhood like any other village boy. Even like any other village boy, whenever I got a chance, I also used to steal fruits from the gardens of other villagers even though same fruits were available in abundance in our own garden. However, probably, I have spoiled my childhood upto a great extent by entering into a competition with my own achievements as a young boy. I always raised my bar for myself which made me a tougher person at the cost of a 'lovely childhood' of a village boy of rural India.

As a student I was very impatient (even now probably) and I could not sit in the same position even for a minute. For this particular bad habit, which still I am having, I used to get at least five sticks a day from a particular teacher when I was in class IV. So, I am perhaps one of the unique students who got more than one thousand sticks in class IV, not for 'fighting with other students', or not for 'not doing homework' or not for 'giving a wrong answer in the class.' I have no grudge for that teacher for those 1000 sticks in a single year, rather feel sorry for him, because he could not change my bad habit despite his constant efforts for a whole year. Still at the age of sixty also, I cannot sit in the same posture for more than ten minutes.

I was a day dreamer, who wanted to do something special for self and others. Unfortunately, I achieved something which was much less than what I dreamt for. For example, in school I took part in all the cultural activities, like recitation, debating, extempore speech, etc. only with moderate success. However, as I grew older, I understood, I was not that intelligent or efficient to achieve something exceptional in all the curricular activities. Then I concentrated only in two activities, reading books and writing short stories. Slowly, I started getting some recognition in the field of writing. Though I could not get an exceptional result in the HSLC examination, I slowly peaked in my subsequent examinations the most so far percentage of marks I had scored. That is my childhood in short.

Chapter II: My Early Life

I got the taste of public humiliation on my very first day of my High School. I have a dubious distinction amongst my family members that only I was not allowed to appear in the scholarship examination (britwi pariksha, an examination for the intelligent students for getting state scholarship when he/she would pass out from Class III to Class IV). Both of my siblings and my parents had appeared in that examination in their respective years as the best students from their respective classes spanning more than three decades. My mother, being the Head Pandit of my school, was in the helm of affairs to select the best student of her school to appear in that examination. However, on the advice of my father, who thought, my selection to the examination would be a big question mark on my mother's integrity, I was not sent for that examination. So, I had to appear in the regular examination of class III in a different school, conducted by a board to be promoted to class IV. Luckily for me, I passed the examination with a first division. Even once someone told me that in that examination, I was able to secure one of the top ten ranks of the whole undivided Darrang district.

I was perhaps little different from most of my classmates and other young boys of my age and therefore many of my relatives and villagers at times because of my apparent foolish statements and actions, used to ridicule me in my childhood days. Many of my classmates were also taunting me at different times till class VI. During the holidays I along with my brother and my classmate uncle, the youngest son of my grandmother (my mother's aunt) used to visit our common maternal uncles' village in our summer vacations. Whenever we three along with one of my cousins (son of my eldest maternal uncle, three months older than I), used to visit any of the relative's place, except me, all were asked, 'what is the course, you are going to take after 12th? Or what is your aim in life?' Probably, all the relatives were more than convinced that I would not be able to cross the barrier of 12th with a good result. One of the pseudo astrologers even once predicted that, I might not cross class-IX examination with one attempt. Of course, still I cannot not find the reason, why all those persons could not see any hope in my face but all could see a bright future in the faces of my brother, cousin and uncle. However, to my surprise, contrary to the common perceptions of most of my relatives and the villagers about me, one teacher (he happens to be a teacher of our entire family except my younger sister) could see something else when I was hardly 5-6 years old. Had that teacher not visited our home and given a pep talk, who knows, my life would have been destroyed beyond repair by my relatives and the villagers.

However, after class VIII (I did not study in class VII), everything had changed so far perceptions of my relatives and our village people me and my IQ level. From then onwards, instead of commenting adversely on me for my apparent foolish comments; most of the people from my locality started finding something extraordinary intellectual in my apparent foolish questions and statements. Villagers started citing my name as the brightest student in the village. From that point onwards, my statements were tried to be deciphered instead of ridiculed even by my teachers. For my apparent foolish questions, my teachers started taking time to answer those questions with utmost caution. I started coming out of the cocoon which I had made for myself till I did something special in class VIII.

But before going to my life after the class VIII examination, let us once again go back to the first day in my new school. On that day, the students were segregated into two groups, those who appeared in the scholarship examination and those who appeared for the regular examination. The students who appeared in the scholarship examination were taken to the room for the elite section and the rest of the students were taken to two different rooms earmarked for the ordinary students. That was my first public humiliation. Luckily for me, a combined examination for all the students, from both categories, was conducted for allotting sections, where I was able to stand first and was able to garner some prestige in the eyes of my teachers for me.

In the next three years as a routine norm, I stood first in all the annual examinations. But that was not enough to shake off my dumb sticker in the eyes of my relatives and the people of my locality. In the eyes of most of my relatives, villagers and teachers, my one-year senior class was full of intelligent boys whereas my class was a class of dumb boys. So, I was considered as the first among a bunch of dumb boys of my class.

But every dog has a day. I was also given an opportunity to hit back, to shake off my dumb sticker by the system itself; or by the Almighty himself? My batch was promoted directly from Class VI to Class VIII as a policy matter of the Government of Assam to squeeze the number of classes in the high school from seven to six. So, I had given an opportunity to compete with the taunted group of intelligent boys one year senior to me. The first examination for the combined class was held after nine months of amalgamation of two classes due to the inability to provide textbooks to the students the Government in time. When the result of the first combined examination was declared, to everyone's surprise, I was able to beat everyone from my combined class. The saga continued all along in my academic career and even in service career as well.

Despite of my mental agony of being taunted as a dumb boy by relatives and by the villagers, I enjoyed my village life to the optimum level; though it cannot be said to a maximum level, because of my self-made pressure to do the best possible results in any examination. During my childhood days, I learned swimming in the dreaded river Mornoi. During the same period, I used to go for fishing, hunting and also used to go for stealing fruits from others' orchards with my friends. Once while stealing plums in one of our uncles' orchards, my elder brother was caught; but my speed of running saved the day for me. However, even after catching red-handed, my elder brother was not thrashed by our uncle for his mischievous act; but was given a full bag of plums with an advice not to steal plums; instead, the uncle invited both of us to their home to eat as many plums as we could eat.

But both of us never followed the good advice of our uncle and the uncle also stopped chasing us as perhaps he also realized that plums and other fruits were not the targets of the children; but 'stealing from others orchard' was done only for enjoyment. For the record, in those days whatever, we along with our friends used to steal from others' orchards were all available in our own orchard and those were distributed among all the children of the village as nothing from our orchard was sold in the market when we were young and even after that, so long our parents were alive.

I had a reasonably good result in the HSLC examination (though that was the second-worst result out of five important examination of my life) and was good enough to get admission into the science stream in Cotton College, the best college of Assam in those days. In class twelfth, I improved my result compared to HSLC and in B.Sc. (H) I could improve my final result a little further. In Masters from Delhi University, I did a horrible result but in my M. Phil I regained my lost ground to get a far better result than I had expected. And in the very first attempt itself, I was able to crack the ISS, UPSC examination and joined into the Central Government as a Class I officer at the age of 23.

As already mentioned, I was a jack of all trades but master of none. Some small successes were also coming my way in my student life in extracurricular activities. I was a regular prize winner in school level competitions in debating, extempore speech, recitation, acting, writing short stories and poems. Just for the record, I even won two first prizes in recitation and direction of one act play in school tournament comprising more than 100 schools.

Because of my extra-curricular activities, a few girls of my age had shown some weakness towards me and with some of them I had been able to make some relations, lasting from one month to a few years. But unfortunately, my wife was not in that category of girls who had any feelings for me.

Perhaps I was a natural leader for at least some of peers and therefore I was elected as the Secretary of the college magazine with a record margin of votes (final score was 666-200 in my favour). During that period, there was agitation against the illegal foreigners, basically those came from the erstwhile East Pakistan and independent Bangla Desh who had settled down mainly in the bank of Brahmaputra.

I initially supported the agitation wholeheartedly as I was convinced by the logic explained by the agitating leaders that, it was the last fight for the Assamese people for preserving their political and cultural identity. But as the agitation progressed for years, I was able to understand, the agitating leaders, might be barring a few, were neither visionary nor they were honest in leading the agitation. Because of the agitation, school and colleges were closed forcefully for almost one year and in the meantime most of the leaders sent their wards outside Assam, some of them even sent their wards to foreign countries to pursue their higher studies un-interrupted.

Realizing that the ordinary students were the only ones being cheated by the leaders for their own interest, I started writing about reopening of schools in a newspaper which was opposing the agitation from the very beginning. The article was appreciated by many and a host of neutral writers supported me for my efforts to reopen the schools. Politicians opposing the agitation bee-lined to recruit me to their folds and pro-agitation leaders threatened my family members in my village, though I was never been threatened by anyone openly.

Finally, schools and colleges were reopened and I passed out from the college with flying colours. Then I not only left Assam and joined Delhi University for my higher studies, but also, I left my writing habits for nearly three decades except writing few guide books for the APSC aspirants.

However, after getting a shock treatment from a senior, again I started my writing career as an English writer. At first, I published my articles/

stories/ poems in the form of ebooks and afterwards started publishing printed books.

So far my career is concerned; I was offered a regular lecturer job in Cotton College, Guwahati after my selection by the Assam Public Service Commission (APSC) in 1985 January. However, due to state politics, I could join into the service in the month of September only. I worked there only for three months as I was already selected by UPSC for a Group-A Central Government job also, as per the result published by UPSC in April, 1985.

During the small period of time of my lectureship in Cotton College, I got a proposal for marriage with a young and a beautiful lady. I did not even take a second before saying 'yes' to the proposal even without meeting her. At that time, I did not know even the family background of her properly. I married her within two months of our first meeting, just nine days before my joining the Indian Statistical Service at New Delhi. As a result of that I could not appear in Civil Service examinations, on a serious note though I could qualify the preliminary examination twice without much ado.

This is my academic career and my marriage in a nutshell; nothing to be proud of, nor anything to be ashamed of.

Chapter III: Humiliation in Career Building

I have explained earlier about my first public humiliations on the first day in my high school. However, after joining into Cotton College, I had to face one humiliation after another one on a daily basis and perhaps it continued my entire life, hopefully unlike many of my esteemed readers. But please do not think all the humiliations meted out to me were intentional; in many cases, the persons did not even know that they were humiliating me by their words and actions. Further, some of the humiliating comments were not targeted against me, but it did hurt me only because I was also similarly placed with the targeted person. For example, one of my hostel boarders commented upon another boarder who happened to be a son of a lecturer of a college, 'what he thinks about himself, I am a son of a principal of a college under whom hundreds of lecturers are working!'

Since I was a son of teacher parents, what he said about the son of a lecturer applied to me also, even worse, perhaps. But yes, in his statement, I was hurt less, but had more pity on the mindset of the son of the Principal of a college.

The word 'gaolia bhoot' or 'gaoburha' (village boy/ rustic) was attached to me being from rural area sometimes hurt me when I was a young man. However, slowly I started enjoying my rural status and I vowed not to change myself into the shoes of an urban elite. In fact, whenever someone taunts me today that I remained 'the gao burha of 1976', I feel proud that even after staying in the urban areas more than four decades, the urbanisation or the urban elite with whom I have to interact day in and day out, could not change me and my style of living. After spending 5 years in Guwahati, I migrated to Delhi for my master degree course. Since 1981 to 1985 I was a student of Delhi University, staying in different types of rented accommodations. The first accommodation was good, as it was little bit costly. The second accommodation was bad and the land lord was worse who even switched off the electricity so that I could not run the fan at 40 plus celsus at night. In fact, I had to appear for my M.Sc final examination without proper sleep at night for the examination period starting from April, 20. The third accommodation was worse than the second one (it was a barsati-a small room which could hardly accommodate a folding cot in winters and in summers I slept in the open); but the owner was a gem of a person. His children, who were of my age, became very good friends of mine in due course of time and we remain friends till today. The wife of the landlord was a very nice lady who treated me as her own son till her death after few years. Because of that, I continued in that accommodation, till I joined the job of Group-A officer in 1985.

Dilliwalla are very fond of humiliating others as lesser human being unless you can impose upon them as seniors or appear more powerful than them. When I reached Delhi from Assam, neither I was powerful nor an imposing young man with sufficient money in my pocket or a boy of well-connected background. Therefore, for not having sufficient money and not having any relative in the city, I was subjected to daily humiliations from shop keepers, landlords (except the last one; even though sometimes one of the children of that landlord used to taunt me occasionally on my financial and rural background) and fellow students from better backgrounds, financially or socially or both.

Chapter IV: The Positive Contributors

The chapter is written about a glorified donkey who became a human being through proper training by some exceptionally talented trainers whom we fondly call as our teachers.

Through this chapter, I want to pay my tributes to some of my revered teachers. However, readers may sometimes feel that it is a self-glorifying story of my own; but in my opinion to understand their greatness, my reference may be essential. In my efforts to submit my obeisance to my teachers, I may have missed many good points of my teachers for which I submit my unconditional apology. Further, I am to clarify that it is not a compilation of biographies of my teachers; rather it is a tribute to some of my teachers by painting some colours by using my own brush. In other words, I am describing my associations with them as per my own perspective only. As I am describing them through my own lenses, I have mentioned in this book whatever I am aware of them and have not done any research beyond my associations with them.

Since I had completed my M. Phil Degree in 1984, I had at least 150 regular teachers in my student life and beyond. Out of these 150 teachers only around 20 teachers influenced me in my career building and in my personal life, rest of the 130 odd teachers had very less or no influence at all in my life including in my career building. On the other hand, another 10 teachers who were not my classroom teachers had influenced my career and my personal life enormously. Therefore, in my tribute, I have mentioned about my take from those informal teachers of my life through our long associations.

Though I was born to a teachers' family, I was scolded by my father, my first management Guru, on a regular basis as 'Gaadha', (a donkey in Assamese) or 'apadartha' (hopeless fellow). Just to understand my background, I want to share few facts before my esteemed readers; not for boasting but to understand the stark reality of my life and my surroundings.

My father's residence was electrified in 1979 when I was doing my graduation in Cotton College. I used to walk for two kms daily bare foot to attend my primary and high school from a very tender age due to some family compulsions. My father's home was provided with tap water connection in 2020. I was the first Science graduate of my family on either side; paternal and maternal. I was the first Master Degree holder of my family on both sides; paternal and maternal. Naturally, I was the first research scholar of the family to be awarded an M. Phil degree by Delhi University. I was the first person to crack UPSC and also, I was the first person of the family to become a lecturer of the most prestigious college of Assam, Cotton College. I was the first person of the family to represent the country in different forums and also, I was the first person of the family to visit many foreign countries. The list of being the first of the family may be very long and therefore I stopped here.

Whatever I have listed as being the first of the family above may be laughable for most of my friends and my colleagues in different offices, I have worked during my long service career. A person with a worse background than mine might be able to achieve much more than what I have achieved in my life. Therefore, nothing exceptional I have done in my life. Then why I am blowing my own trumpets before you for so long?

The reason why I am blowing my own trumpet is; without saying those things, readers may not realize whatever I have achieved in my life till today (may not be great in anyone's eyes), it is because of my revered teachers from class one to the M. Phil degree in the University. Without their support and teachings, I could not have achieved anything in my life. I shall be always thankful to each and every teacher in my life. I have mentioned here only few of them; perhaps I missed some of them; but I am thankful to all of them and I submit my apology for missing anyone's name.

My mother was the first teacher of my life as she was the Head Pandit (gender neutral word) of the primary school where I started my formal schooling of my life. Naturally, I learnt first lesson of management from my father who also happened to be a Head Master of a high school. Therefore, the relation between me and my teachers had to be started from my third teacher, Ganesh Goswami Sir, in my lower primary school. He was an angry young man and was known for his good teaching skills and also is infamous for his uncontrolled anger. As I was good in mathematics, I had little problem in dealing with Goswami sir during two years' of association with him. But I was very bad in other subjects and most importantly, I used to commit lot of spelling mistakes while writing (in Assamese). However, I had never been beaten up for my spelling mistakes by sir, might be because of being the son of the Head Pandit or because of my exceptional receptive power in mathematics.

In the high school, I was taught by almost thirty odd teachers; out of which I still fondly remember the names of few teachers; Mahendra Barkataki sir, fondly called him as the Head Sir by the students, Swarnalata Mahanta Madam (for her belief in me), Jiten Barkataki Sir (for his management skill), Tarun Saikia sir (change of my attitude towards life), Leela Katoky Sir (giving me the basic knowledge in English), Nishi Bordoloi sir (instrumental in building my confidence), Narayan Das Sir (infusing mathematics in my blood), Ramen Boruah sir (infusing romantic thinking in my heart), Sarbeswar Hazarika Sir (infusing scientific thinking in my head), Anil Sharma sir, Golap Hazarika Sir, Binoy Bora sir and Chota Miya sir (he was my first spiritual guru). However, I cannot forget love for me by Hari Prasad Upadhya sir (infusing liking for history) and S. Charaborty sir (I learnt story telling from him) and M. Upadhaya sir (Sanskrit). My own uncle, Jiten Bora sir also taught me during my school days. Rest of the teachers had very less influence in my career building. Except one teacher, who tried to teach me drawing (he was the carpentry teacher) and who failed measurably to improve my capability in improving my drawing skill, was the only teacher who slapped me in my entire student career. However, I forgot his name which I seldom do normally and glad to do in this particular case.

In Cotton College during my student's life, there were around 140 teachers as professors and lecturers in different departments. Since I was elected the Editor of 'Cottonian' in 1979-80, during the publication of the magazine, I had the opportunity to meet many sirs and madams who had not taught me in my regular classes. However, during that period, I had developed a very good relation with many of them and learnt many good things from them.

In Delhi University, I was a non-entity and my result in M.Sc. also did not come very handy to make good relation with majority of the teaching staff of Delhi University. However, thanks to one of the sirs, Prof. Sudhendu Biswas, I was able to bounce back and for that I owe him for my present status, whatever it is good or bad.

Please do not think that I have no respect for the other teachers of Delhi University. I always remember magnificent class room teachings of Prof. S. C. Gupta sir and Prof. Kanwar Singh sir. We, all the students of master degree of my class used to admire the efforts of Prof. Jagdish Singh Saran sir and Veena Agarwal Madam while teaching us. Prof. Saroj Alawaidi Madam's untimely death gave lot of pain in my heart when

I was working in Social Statistics Division of CSO, Ministry of Statistics and Programme Implementation. After leaving the University, I was able to make good rapport with Prof. Ashok Basal sir and Prof. M. C. Aggarwal sir and we had met many times as professionals in different committees of Government of India.

In the next few paragraphs I try to recall some of my revered teachers and their contributions in building my personality and career.

High School Teachers:

Swarnalata Mahanta, popularly known as Swarna Baideu was the Assistant Head Master when I was admitted in the class IV of Chatia Boys' High School, the school, where except my younger sister Minakshi, everyone in my family had studied upto class X. She had never taken any class of mine, as she used to teach in the higher class only and then, she left the school to fight an election for Legislative Assembly of Assam when I was in class VI. Not only did she won the election, but she also became one of the Ministers of Assam in the Sarat Chandra Sinha Cabinet in 1972. If she had not taken any class of mine when I was a student in that school, then how did she became one of the most revered teachers for me? Is it because she taught my parents? The answer was a resounding 'no'.

It all started at a seminar where I had presented a paper on Sankar Deb; the most revered Religious Guru of Assam on his death Anniversary, popularly known in Assam as 'Sankar Deb-ar Tirobhav Tithi'. I was the youngest student, at class IV who had presented a paper in presence of the entire students and teachers of the school. After presentation of the paper, she gave me a bear hug and blessed me with the following remark, 'I am proud of you, Borah Sahab. Keep it up.'

I was surprised at her address as she used to address my father as 'Bharat', mother as, 'Dashami' and my elder brother as 'Apurba' as all of them were students of Swarna Baideu alongwith me. In the subsequent meetings with her in any school functions and at the corridor of the school she always asked me with a smile, 'How are you Borah Sahab? How are Bharat and Dashami?'

That question and that address of Swarna Baideu always echoes in my mind, whenever I am addressed by someone as 'Borah Sahab' instead of 'Hiranya' or 'Borah jee' or with a simple 'Borah.' To my surprise as of today ninety percent of Non-Assamese people address me as Borah Sahab (Saab) or simply address me, 'sir'. Therefore, I have no alternative but to ask myself sometimes, 'Was she able to see my future before I attained the age of ten that I would be living outside Assam and holding a reasonably good post which would be the factor to be addressed as Borah Sahab?'

I am not sure about that; but there was one link about her address and about the comments of Tikani Mastar (who commented before my mother that I am going to outshine all my ancestors, though I am yet to outshine any of my ancestors on any parameters) on me. Swarna Baideu was the younger sister of Tikani Mastar. Like her brother, was she able to see something in me, unusual of a village rustic boy?

Whatever might be the reason of calling me 'Borah Sahaab' at an age below ten, she infused confidence in my mind to think about myself that I was a cut above my peers and time; I would be able to do something what many people would not be able to do. That is why I consider her as one of the Gurus, who tried to put me in the group of elites; though I am not sure actually where I stand today.

'Kimaan pabi o lora (what is your expectation/ what you are expecting to score, my child)?' I still vividly remember each and every sentence of Saikia sir and the situation in the room on that day until today.

With a stick in his hand Tarun Saikia sir asked me. Tarun Saikia sir, popularly known as Hindi sir, like Swarna Baideu was the Hindi sir for my parents, elder brother and me as well. He was a teacher for me from class IV to VI, as after Class VIII (I did not study in class VII) Hindi was not compulsory in the schools of Assam. Whatever my proficiency in Hindi (I happened to be nodal officer of the Hindi Department/ Ministry of Drinking Water and Sanitation at the later part of my career), I am always indebted to him and whatever inefficiency in my Hindi speaking capacity remained with me till date, it is because of my non-serious approach for any of the subjects I had learnt throughout my life.

On that particular day, many students had already been punished by sir, for not doing well in the half yearly examination of class VI while returning their answer-scripts. Till that year, my friend Om Prakash Aggarwal used to get highest marks in Hindi in all the examinations as a routine matter. Except Hindi and Drawing, I used to maintain a steady progress in all the other subjects. Sir had already handed over the answer-script of Om Prakash with a score of 64. Therefore, I was thinking about a score in between 60 to 64 for me in that examination. But his question put me in a very difficult position. I thought, since he was asking me the question of my expectation, I might have scored an extremely bad mark in that examination. I preferred to keep mum.

To my horror, he picked up the stick to a height with which he could have hit me with enormous force. I closed my eyes in fear for a moment. The stick hit my shoulder softly and I heard the soft and caring voice of Hindi sir, 'why you do not have confidence in your ability? You have everything to excel in your life; but I feel sometimes you are still lacking some confidence in yourself to do something great.'

He handed over my answer-script to my trembling hands. On that day I realize, I was able to beat a favourite person or an apparently unbeatable person with my own efforts and ability. Actually, sir was delighted at my progress in Hindi alongwith other subjects over the years. Naturally, I was delighted to see my marks on the top of the answer script, 73/100. It was not a great score as of today's standard and even in my own standard as I used to score more than 80% marks in all other subjects except Drawing and Assamese. But I was delighted to see my steady progress in the subject where I was really very bad when I started my learning in Hindi language in the half yearly examination of class IV. I was able to score only 1/10 in the spelling part; I distinctly remember that I could correctly spell only one word 'Ganga' and spelling of all other words were found to be incorrect. From that position, within two years, I was able to score the highest marks in the class beating a Hindi speaking student; all credit goes to my teacher, Tarun Saikia sir.

Further, his statement on that day on my attitude towards my own life, helped me in developing confidence to do something for me and for my society. I shall always be thankful to sir for those words even after decades of his death.

Recently his son who was two years senior to me, Shri Madan Saikia reminded me how much he used to love me as his student and as a son of two favoured students, my father and my mother. Incidentally, his eldest son Ranjit Saikia was one of the most favourite students of my father, Bharat Chandra Borah.

When I was a student of that high school during the period of 1970-76, Late Jiten Barkataki Sir was the Assistant Head Master of Chatia Boys' High School after Swarnalata madam left the school to start her political journey. Sir went on to become the Principal of the Chatia Higher Secondary School once Chatia Boys' High School was upgraded to a Higher Secondary School. Incidentally, he was the second Principal of the Higher Secondary after Late Shri Mahendra Barkataki Sir.

Late Shri Jiten Barkataki sir had never taken any regular class of mine because his second son, Shri Pranab Barkataki was in my class from class

IV to Class X. Therefore, I think; I was one of the few unlucky students of Chatia Boys' High School who were deprived of his teachings on regular basis. On the other hand, my elder brother, Dr. Apurba Borah and my parents were lucky to be his students with regular classes to be taken by Barkataki sir during their school days. However, I was also lucky to have some teachings from him whenever he used to take a class of mine as a stop gap arrangement when any of our regular teachers were not in a position to take our class on a given day.

I was always awed with his much above average personality with a height of six feet and with a muscular body. He was always in his spotless white dhoti- Punjabi while attending school for taking classes of his students. His personality itself was a source of inspiration for all of us.

However, I always remember Barakataki sir as one of my first management teachers as a student of management in the entire life (should I mention that I got a short stint of management training in IIM Lucknow, Royal University of Melbourne and University of Sydney). His management technique helped me in my service career from a junior Direct Recruit Group-A Central Government Officer to the present capacity as a Senior Officer in Government of India. How without uttering a single word on management, he taught me his first lesson of management (after my own father has taught me management in day to day life) to control subordinates, in general and those who were close to me due to some social relations with them, in particular. Let us find out how I learnt management from Barakataki sir in the following paragraphs.

When I was in class IV, I used to sit with Pranab on the same bench accommodating four-five students of different calibre as per the arrangement made by the class teacher. Normally we used to sit on the first bench of left side of the room and right side of the teacher facing the class. I used to sit at the aisle seat and Pranab used to sit next to my seat on regular basis. Whenever sir used to take our class, after teaching something, he would pose a question to all of us. Instead of asking any question directly to any student, he posed the question to the student sitting at the window seat of the first bench where incidentally I also used to sit alongwith Pranab. Luckily or unluckily that particular student seldom was able to give a correct answer to the satisfaction of sir. Then his most important learning session started for me.

Then without looking at the face of the student, he used to utter the word, 'next.'

Fortunately or unfortunately, the next student also usually used to fail to answer the question correctly posed by sir. Then, Barkataki sir used to utter again the same word, ‘next’ without looking at the face of the student. The third / fourth student happened to be his son Pranab. Pranab used to give the answer, most of the time correctly. Then sir would utter the same word, ‘next’ and would pose a new question to me if Pranab had given a correct answer, otherwise the same question would be repeated for me as well.

In his next step, the second part of my management teaching came to me automatically. Whenever Pranab failed to answer the question correctly and if I was able to answer the question correctly, all the three students including Pranab were punished. Corporal punishment given by a teacher in those days was very common unlike today when a teacher dares not to give any corporal punishment to a student.

However, whenever I also failed to answer the question, the question was thrown open to all the students for giving the correct answer. Fortunately for me (I am not boasting), 99% of those questions were unanswered by any of my classmates. Then sir would explain the answer of the question so nicely, still I could remember all the nuances of the questions and answers. In a sense, whenever I could give the correct answers and Pranab failed, all the three students including Pranab used to get punished. In those days, as a young boy I could not follow properly why he used to do so. But when I looked back after holding some important posts in different organizations, the whole strategy of sir became crystal clear to me.

Sir directly did not want to ask Pranab any question to test the level of his learning in the class. But whenever I failed to answer the question correctly, he used to think that the whole class might have some problem in understanding about the question or about the chapter from which the question had been asked. In either of the case, he wanted to make it clear to all the students about the chapter through his experienced teachings. During my entire school days, so far as I remember, I had never been punished by sir.

When I was posted at Guwahati as the Head of the Office of NSSO for the entire North East Region except Meghalaya and Tripura, I had to control persons who used to have some other relations beyond official relations. For example, one of the officers who happened to be the elder brother of one of my teachers in Cotton College had to report to me as his immediate boss. Another officer who used to claim that he was one year senior to my father in Darrang College, had also reported to me as his immediate superior. Another officer who was two steps below me, used to call Apurba and his wife by name. In the initial years of my service, more than ninety percent of my subordinates in any office were older than me in age. I had to control them and had to take work from them on day to day basis. Then I remembered how sir had controlled his own son in the class without showing any biasedness towards him.

In that particular office, within a very short time, I was able to identify a group of efficient officers, whom I made the threshold of doing any work efficiently like sir did in identifying me as the threshold of understanding of a chapter to be explained once again or not. Whenever, I had to deal with some known people in my career, I always remember sir fondly.

For the last few years, as I have been appointed as the nodal officer of the then Ministry of Drinking Water and Sanitation and now rejigged as Department of Drinking Water and Sanitation, Ministry of Jalshakti for the entire North East in implementing the Swachh Bharat Mission, Gramin, I have to interact with the State Departments in implementing the SBM (Gramin) in their states. Due to divergent work culture in different states, I had to face lots of challenges in dealing with the officers of different states. So far Assam is concerned, as many of the senior officers of the State Government were my classmates in Cotton College and many were senior to me in my college, my problem in dealing with them has been more challenging compared to other States and UTs of India. Thanks to the early management training of sir, somehow, I have been able to manage to motivate the concerned people to deliver the best of their abilities in their allotted duties with the help of those senior officers of the states without any problem. I am always thankful to all of those officers alongwith Borkotoky sir and some other teachers, for making my work easier in implementing a scheme which is very close to the heart of the Honourable Prime Minister of India.

Leela Katoky sir made the foundation of my English learning when I joined the school as a student of class IV in 1970. The basic grammar what he taught to me has been the foundation of my writing capability in English. In fact, my 93/100 in my first examination in the half yearly examination cleared the path of mine to make me think differently from other students of my class. 97/100 in mathematics only consolidated my position at the top of my class. Readers may think the marks were not very convincing for my boastful thinking of a better student. But in 1970 these were considered to be good marks as the second highest marks in my class hovers in the range of 70-80 only. Therefore, if my teachers saw something in me, it was because of teachings in English of Shri Leela Katoky sir in class IV and my relatively better grasping power in mathematics.

Shri Nishi Bordoloi sir made me confident as a good student in English when I was in class V. In those days Nishi sir used to teach English in class V-A (my class) as a class teacher and also used to take classes in English for the students of Class IX- C in the sixth period. Sixth period was the drawing class for me. Therefore, Nishi sir used to take me to the English class of Class IX to teach grammar to the senior students of class IX in his presence. Practically that gave me so much confidence that I started reading the English text books of class IX when I was in class V. However, that gave me some headache during my examination days. In those days due to paucity of accommodation, four students of different classes were allowed to sit on the same bench. In the process whoever sat on my bench, if he was not a good student, he used to ask me to help him irrespective of the subjects he was appearing for and irrespective of class he belonged to. Of course, today I enjoy those moments of glory and submit my thanks to Nishi Sir for making me special in those days.

Narayan Das sir made me feel good in mathematics. He used to ask me after explaining a new chapter in mathematics, 'can you understand what I have taught?' If I would say a 'no' he used to explain again and again so long I would say a 'yes' to sir. However, in 90% cases, I used to say 'yes' on his first attempt. In rare one or two cases in his three years of my association with Narayan Das sir, he had to explain me more than twice. Once, I would say a 'yes' rest of the time, I was given the duty to explain, if anyone needed help in understanding the process. My involvement in the teaching process helped me to understand the process neatly. Those processes are still in my mind till today.

Chota Miya sir taught me simple living and high thinking. Recently I remembered Chota Miya sir with lot of respect due to a small incident that involved me unwittingly. The incident evolved as under:

'Bhaiya, Pandara Road ka B-30 kaha parega (Where is B-30 of Pandara Road)?' Few years ago, three young boys, about 19-20 asked me in Hindi when I was carrying two heavy bags to my residence after alighting from the metro station located at Khan Market, New Delhi.

I told the direction to the youngsters. I did not mind, though I was not 100% sure, if my ego was not bruised, when the young boys addressed me as a 'Bhaiya', a derogatory address for a well-educated person like me. However, 'Bhaiya' is also an address for an elder brother within the family members. In that particular case, they did not address me as their elder brother, as in reality, I might be even older than their parents. But I did not become angry with them; rather, I was amused that they might have thought me as a labourer or something like that; as I was sure that they did not think me little older than them.

Though, I was new to that place at that time, I had already noticed, that normally, a very few well to do pedestrians were seen on that street. Most of the pedestrians on that street were mostly, daily wage earners or CPWD's manual workers or students or the family members living in the servant quarters attached to the Government Quarters for the senior officers. Therefore, their address to me as Bhaiya, not as uncle or sir might be perfectly justified. As, all of us know that in India, 'Dignity of Labour' is the first causality in the public places.

However, what followed next had disturbed me a lot more. All three boys appeared to be from good family background and that was really worrisome for all of us. They were walking about five feet ahead of me and thinking (probably) I was an illiterate, they freely, with pretty loud voices, were discussing about a common friend, using the dreaded four letter (F...) word quite frequently, ignoring very existence of an old (or young) fellow like me. There might be two reasons of ignoring me, one, they might have the perception, that I was an illiterate person and two; they didn't bother, very existence of any other fellow, irrespective of his age, background etc. The second perception was probably more dangerous.

That reminded me an old incident involving Late Chota Mian Sir, who taught me English in class VIII. He was an extremely simple, but very learned man and on principle, he had never put on any shoe or chappal on his feet and always clad in Dhoti and Kurta.

The railway line connecting Tezpur (Rangapara) and Jonai (North Lakhimpur) was crossing a village named as 'Ghahi Gaon' in Chatia Subdivision of Sonitpur District of Assam. Sir used to take a short cut to school which was along the train line.

One fine morning, he saw a crowd assembled on the train line looking at a tom-tom car. When he approached the place where the crowd had been gathered, he saw a tom- tom car with two railway officials on it. The officials were inspecting the track. But reaching the place, he felt very bad as the two officials were talking in English and criticizing the crowd in an extremely derogatory manner. After listening to them for few minutes, in chaste English, he asked the officials, should he translate their observations on the villagers to Assamese.

For a moment, they were shell shocked and in the following moments, with folded hands, they apologized for their words and requested Sir, not to translate what they were saying about the villagers. Sir did not translate those sentences, but advised them not to repeat the same mistake in future.

I hoped, they had never repeated any such type of mistakes in the rest of their lives.

I told this story many a times to my children, so that, they do not underestimate any person by looking at his dress or on the basis of his / her background, colour or any other reasons.

I also always advise my children when they were young to keep in mind that anything objectionable should not be spoken in public by using English language which may be counterproductive at many a time.

It is also a fact that, in India, unfortunately intelligence of a person is judged by English speaking capacity. It is nothing but a colonial mentally inherited from the British Raj in India. I was blessed to visit a few non-English speaking countries where progress in industrial sectors and other scientific sectors were far ahead of India or any other South Asian countries where English has been spoken amongst the elites. We normally conveniently forget that English is nothing but a language only to communicate our minds to another person like any other language. However, I agree that English is the lingua franca for most of the countries in the world; but it is also equally important to remember that English is not the most spoken language in the world.

You might be thinking that I had an excellent result in my HSLC final after showing so much potential in my class examination. In fact, my HSLC result with 68% was only the second worst among the five final examinations that I had appeared (M. Sc final examination had been the worst) in my student life. Fortunately, however for me, that percentage was enough to score the highest marks among the successful candidates from Chatia HSLC centre in that year comprising of nine schools and enough to get a seat in the science stream in Cotton College comfortably for my higher studies. For that particular year 68% marks was enough to secure a National Merit Scholarship which continued till my Master Degree because of two back to back good results in Class XII and B.Sc. (H).

You may have developed a feeling after reading upto this point that I was loved by all the teachers equally in the school. That was also a wrong notion. One of my class teachers who taught me Assamese literature in the first period used to take history class also in the fourth period from Monday to Friday. He used to punish me by hitting me with a stick following a beautiful criterion made by him: if I was beaten in the first period; that did not guarantee me that I would not be beaten up in the fourth period. But fortunately, or unfortunately if I was not beaten up in the first period, he made a point to beat me up in the fourth period more vigorously.

His disliking for me was so much so that he had given me in Assamese and History so low marks (less than fifty in both the papers, precisely 49/100 and 42/100) resulting my overall marks less than another boy by two marks in the first half yearly examination. He even did not give me marks for correct answers in 'fill up the gaps' questions citing that my handwriting was not upto the mark. He played the same tricks in the annual examination also. But my friend could not cope up the heat of the competition in the rest of the examinations and faded out from the next examination itself. Finally in the final HSLC examination he got a mere third division. Again in the class V half yearly examination, the Drawing Teacher (who was the only teacher to slap me) gave 32/100 (against giving 75/100 to the second boy) so that I cannot hold the first position (with the sole aim to demoralize me). Similarly, in the class ten half yearly examination, the English teacher gave me 44/100 by giving 'zero/ 1' marks in all the descriptive questions. In fact, I got almost cent percent marks in the grammar and less than 10 % marks in the descriptive section. To humiliate me further, he gave better marks to a boy than mine who was once expelled in one of the earlier examinations for cheating. However, as expectedly that friend of mine also got a third Division in the final examination and faded out from my radar permanently in due course of time. Behaviour of these two teachers was two extreme examples only. Few other teachers were also playing some dirty tricks against me taking the cover of secrecy which I could know only after few years of leaving the school from a teacher who used to love me from his heart without any reservation.

However, those teachers who were constantly playing their tricks to spoil my career had their last laugh when I was awarded 61/100 only in the work experience paper in the final examination of class X against awarding79/100 to two students who according to them had the potential to beat me with their helping hands, as that was the only paper which was assessed in the school itself. I have nothing against the two students who happened to be my good friends for getting better marks than I in work experience; but I have lot of grievances about the school authority who backstabbed me by telling in public that, 'I should bring laurel to our school' and awarding a mark which was in their hands in such a way that my percentage came down by two percent overall than overall marks of two of my friends. Unfortunately for those teachers, I was able to comprehensively beat both of them despite of all the tricks played against me by those crooked teachers. As expectedly in XII examination I was able to beat them by a margin of more than 10% marks over all. In other words, I got more than 100 marks over all to the next boy of my class who passed out from Chatia Boys' High School in 1976.

Nevertheless, I am always thankful to most of my revered teachers of LP and high school for showing their faith in my mental capability to do something big in my life. I am also thankful to those teachers who planted one plot after another one to break my confidence or to spoil my career unethically during my six years' of high school learning. Actually by doing all sort of nuisance in my early career by those teachers, they indirectly taught me how one should be cautious in life and how to avoid backstabbing. However, I think; I could not avoid backstabbing at any part of my life despite of those early lessons of those teachers in my life. I do not want to mention the names of those teachers because they played all those dirty games against me not because of my 'not so beautiful face' or not due to ill behaviour from my side towards them at any point of time during the entire period of my schooling. They did it because of local politics where on one side my father was standing along with some poor people and on the other side; a group of teachers of my school were standing along with a powerful lobby who had been brooding for my father's blood in his entire life.

I could have been admitted in the high school which was established by my father few years before I was admitted into class IV in my school;

but my mother thought otherwise for both of her sons. She thought; the son of Brihshpati should always study in the school of Shukracharya so that if her son would be able to excel, the whole world would notice his calibre or otherwise he would be perished to ignominy. She took the risk of sending her two sons to a mine field where her sons have to fight for their survival on every day. I do not know, whether I have achieved something through that dogmatic thought process of my mother or not, but I am sure; my schooling in the opposite camp of my father made the donkey inside me to a street dog who can fight for every ounce of flesh on the street. Therefore, I love all the teachers of my high school with different degree of emotions for diametrically opposite reasons.

My Teachers in College:

After my admission to Cotton College, I realized that I was nothing but an extremely ordinary student amongst some of the most intelligent students of contemporary Assam. The feeling of a good student was evaporated from the very first day of attending classes; particularly after attending the first English class taken by Prof. Pradeep Acharya sir. After hearing his explanation on 'Ozymandias of Egypt' I told to myself, 'you fool, who told you to come to Cotton College for your higher studies. None can stop you from drowning in the whirlpool.'

My problem was compounded in manifolds due to comfortable interactions of some of the students with sir, who passed out from English medium schools like Don Bosco of Guwahati. In fact on that night I could not sleep at all. However, on the third day one small incident involving sir and a student from village background had changed all the impression for Acharya sir and Cotton College, particularly about the English Department of Cotton College.

On that day, a boy from rural background dared to ask a question to sir in a rustic way to explain once again as he could not follow what sir was explaining in the class. Some of the students passing out of English medium schools started laughing and making fun of the pronunciations of the student and as a result of their unfriendly behaviour, the student became more nervous. At that moment, sir came down from the podium and put his hands on the shoulders of the students and told the nervous student, 'do not worry. I also used to speak like you when I came to this college few years ago as a student.' I am not sure whether sir was actually telling a truth on that day or not; but that sentence infused lot of confidence in me and inspired many students like me who came to Cotton College to try their luck. And then he scolded the students who laughed at the student for his rustic pronunciation in English.

I do not want to tell the name of the student; but later on he became a professor of a college and has been teaching English for more than three decades with a Ph. D. degree in his kitty; as after two years that particular student preferred to leave science stream and took English as his Honours subject in his degree course. No doubt, he had excellent marks in English in XII final. In due course of time, however those English speaking students also became good friends of mine.

Though I could not excel in English like that particular boy, from that incident, I got the first dose of confidence to continue my studies in Cotton College. However, after declaration of the result of the first terminal examination, I realized that I took a good decision to study in Cotton College.

In the next few months, I had the opportunity to meet Navakanta Borah sir, Prof. Robin Goswami sir, Prof. Upen Sharma sir, Prof. Bhabesh Sarma Sir and Prof. Basanta Boruah sir personally and they told me specifically not to be swayed away by my friends' English speaking capacity. One day, Goswami sir told me when I met him in the common room of the English Department, 'Ultimately your knowledge in English will be judged through your writing capacity; not by your speaking capability.'

At that time, however, sir did not know that I was not very good in English even in writing. Anyway, I did not fail in English paper in class XII as well as in B.Sc final examination and I was also able to pass my graduation in English medium to relief of my parents and to the delight of myself.

In due course of time, I had developed an excellent rapport with Prof. Preeti Rekha Kakati Madam of English Department and she helped me a lot at my personal level. I am always thankful to her for her timely help as her own younger brother when I cleared my UPSC examination and could not get the police verification done of one year of my stay at Guwahati due to some misunderstandings on the part of Guwahati Police. Actually they thought one set of police verification was sufficient for the entire period but actually two separate verifications were required by Government of India as per their protocol. Madam helped me by impressing the police through her husband who was a sitting MP (Member of Parliament) at that time to send the police verification of that particular year and eased out my tension of getting my appointment letter.

In any case, I shall remain grateful to all the teachers of English Department for those encouraging pep talks to me in those depressing days of my life. As a tribute to my revered teachers of the English Department, I was able to score more than 66% marks in English while qualifying in my ISS examination conducted by UPSC after few years down the line.

During 5 years of stay in Cotton College, I was privileged to learn many lessons from many stalwarts of different subjects. Unlike due to bitter politics in our school at Chatia, I did not feel any suffocation in Cotton College and therefore, I did not face any problem in getting best of the teachings, advices, and suggestions and in many cases personal help from my teachers of Cotton College. I always admit; because of their selfless unconditional support I was able to consolidate my career building activities in that phase of my life. I still remember my Gurus (teachers) of Cotton College and their contributions in my career building. Due to their good advices and teachings, I was able to improve my results in the subsequent final examinations. However, probably about twenty of my teachers have more contributions than others and out of these twenty teachers few had never taught me in regular classes; but without their contributions in my career building, I would not have reached the position what I was holding before retirement.

One of my most beloved teachers, Kamala Choudhury Baideu used to love me as her younger brother and I always remember her for her scolding for not doing my viva well in my viva-voce in the internal examination of my B.Sc (Hons). Thanks to her verbal thrashing on that day, that made me a more determined student. Incidentally I had never cut a sorry figure in any of my interviews that followed that internal viva-voce on that day. In fact, I had never failed in any of the interviews I had faced post thrashing of Kamala Baideu on that evening on the Veranda of Statistics Department of Cotton College. Not only I respect her as my teacher, but also I always love her as my elder sister.

Another Guru, Biswajit Chakraborty sir, taught me to see the society in a different perspective. He infused the gender parity in my mind which helped me to become a gender expert in the later part of my life.

Another Guru, who did not teach me in my regular classes, Prof. Satyen Choudhury sir, taught me many things beyond class room education. Incidentally his wife, Sovita Madam who is an elder sister of my classmate, Kalyan Pathak, a renowned legal luminary of India, became my real elder sister in the last four decades of my association with her. Thankfully, their three daughters also treat me as their elder brother in all practical purposes.

Another stalwart, Nabakanta Borah sir taught me to think big in my life. I will not forget how pointing from his car while I was a newcomer in Delhi to the Parliament he said, 'I want you should be there representing Assam one day.' Unfortunately I could not represent Assam so far, but still I had to visit Parliament building as a senior officer many times to assist the concerned ministers for their star parliament questions. Ainu, elder daughter of sir is a good friend of mine. Her husband, Udyan Hazarika aka Utpal is also a close friend of mine.

Another stalwart of Physics, Principal Gobinda Deka sir taught me how to be humble even when holding some very powerful post. He also did not take any regular class of mine. His son, Ajay Deka was a friend of mine and because of our friendship I was privileged to stay in his residential Quarters for few days when our hostel was shut by the administration due to Assam agitation.

Prof. Shyama Prasad Sharma sir also guided me in my life in many ways like a true mentor when I was the Editor of the magazine of Cotton College.

Prof. Tarkeswr Choudhury sir was not only our mathematics teacher but also an uncle of one of my classmates, Dr. Ganesh Choudhury who retired recently as the Vice Principal of Arya Vidyapeeth College of Guwahati. Because of two relations, he played a role of a mentor throughout my life. No doubt, he was an excellent communicator with each and every student he had taught in his long career.

Prof. Bapu Krishna Choudhury sir and Prof. Durga Das sir both have different style of teachings; but both of them used to call me as 'Bapa' and addressed me as 'Toi' instead of 'Tumi' as if I was a son to them. Whenever I remember them, my eyes become moist like remembering my diseased parents.

As mentioned earlier, one of my subordinate officers at Guwahati office was elder brother of one of my teachers in Cotton College. One day when I met him in his Department he asked me, 'Hiranya, where you are working now?'

'Sir, I am working at NSSO, Government of India?'

'Do you know---? He is my elder brother.'

'I did not know sir that he is your elder brother; but I know him very well, sir.' With a low voice I replied.

'Are you working under him?' Sir asked me with a twinkle in his eyes.

'No sir. He is working at Jorhat and I am posted at Guwahati sir.' I replied to his question without mentioning that actually his elder brother was working under me in those days.

After one month, I met sir once again in his department. With his lovely smile he asked me, 'why you did not tell me that you are my elder brother's boss?'

I did not have an answer to his question. On seeing me mum, he told me, 'You made all of us proud. You could have told me on that day itself that you are the boss of my elder brother.'

Then he told all the teachers present there about my silence on that day. On that day, Durga Das sir was also present in the Chemistry Department. He called me near to him and slapped me lovingly and told, 'toi bar badmash lora o' (you are still a very naughty boy.'

I only touched the feet of Das sir like any other dutiful student.

You will be interested to know who the younger brother of my subordinate was in those days. He was none other than Prof. Robin Talukdar sir. Sir made me realized that a student for a teacher is also like a son for a father who want to see his/ her students to grow leaps and bound without any personal gain for the teacher.

I also still fondly recall my Chemistry sir, Prof. Kamaleswer Choudhury sir for his scolding in Chemistry practical classes in class XII for not finding the ring in the test tube like my other elite students who used to get it comfortably. No doubt, those elite friends become teachers in

Chemistry in different reputed colleges including Cotton College or holding some very high post in some premier institutions of India, like IIT or very high post in some research organizations like DRDO or in Indian space Programme. I am always very happy for their success in their professional life and being an average student of Cotton College, I am always very proud to be a classmate of those extremely intelligent students in Class XI and XII.

Prof. Indra Bhatta sir was a teacher of Zoolgy and I did not have that subject in college. Therefore, he was not a regular teacher of mine. But I always remember, Prof. Indra Bhatta sir for his guts to face any eventuality in life and his helping attitude towards the students like me who did not have their home at Guwahati and also had no local guardians at Guwahati to provide any help in emergency. He was always ready to help those marooned students like me of Cotton College.

Prof. Dilip Sharma sir was very young when I was a student in Cotton College. Despite his young age he was extremely good in teaching. I always remember him not only as a good teacher but also as a good big brother even after leaving the college long back. After few years of leaving my college when I have to interact with him for some projects his one sentence always, I fondly remember, 'Hiranya, I do not know whether you have any other work or not, but I cannot understand how you can emerge at the right time at the right place as decided by me.' Sir was right; I cannot make any of my teachers to wait for even a single minute for me. I learnt for this particular habit from my mother's boss Shri Abani Bhagwati, B. Sc(H), the then Principal, Sootea Normal Practicing School at very young age. The story goes like this:

My mother, who was the 'Head Pandit' (Head Master of a Middle School) had to report to Bhagawati sir at that period of time.

As a rural daughter-in law, she had to do all her household chores including rearing of animals and husking of paddy etc. before going to school. Despite of her best efforts, she sometimes failed to reach the school by five minutes or even less in time as the school was situated two kilometer away from our home and she had to travel on foot the entire distance every day. But for her it was a short distance as she had to travel every day eight kilometers, one way, every day as a student. From a very tender age, may be two and a half years I, along with my elder brother Apurba, who was one year, three months' older than I, accompanied our mother to the school. I need not have to mention here that , there was no crèche facility at that time and maternity leave for a working lady in Government was only 2 and a half months. There was a large field in the school, where we used to play with animals and stray boys and girls who never attended school in those days.

Whenever, my mother was late, the Principal used to show his watch pointing towards my mother and some times, he murmured, 'what example, you are going to set before your young children?'

When, I was about five year old, one day, he invited me to his chamber and told me, 'I know, your mother always try to come in time to the school, but she is not able to do it because she may not be very good in time management (probably, he said some other words), so when you will grow, be careful, so that, no boss can show the watch, he is wearing, for your late coming. Always try to reach school/college/office before your teacher/boss reach the class/ office. Then, only you can aspire for bigger success.'

Still, I remember his voice and his advice which had been encrypted in my memory with awe and fear. That is the reason, why I report for my duties much before the designated time, as far as possible.

Further, keeping in my mind, the plight of my mother for attending school and household chores, I am always, sympathetic to all my subordinate young mothers and so far, I am yet to scold any young mother for her late coming for which, many a times, I used to get flaks from my seniors and male colleagues of those young mothers. But still, I had been helping the young mothers as far as possible and I think, that is the only way to show my token of respect to my departed mother.

Anyway, so far time management is concerned; many people ask me a common question where I get time to write so many books with so much responsibility in office. I jokingly I use to tell them, 'God has given me 120 hours in a day instead of 24 hour.' In fact probably, I am little better in time management than an average man and for that I shall always thankful to Abani Bhagwati sir for his pep talk when I was hardly five year old.

In a lighter vein, I must also mention about one of the teachers of Cotton College, name of him is avoided for obvious reason, taught me how one should keep one's libido intact till the age of retirement; fulfilling all other duties of life. Many of my friends will be able to identify that particular professor, at least who follow him in letter and spirit at our age.

Finally, I cannot forget the help of Prof. Biswajit Bhagawati sir for reminding a specific rule of Guwahati University to Prof. Baruah sir, Head of the Statistics to sort out a problem relating to my B.Sc final examination.

Prof. J. Baruah sir was the Head of the Department of Statistics, Cotton College when I met him for the first time as a Pre-university student in 1976. At that time, his personality never allowed me to be closer to him. But situation had changed drastically when I joined as Statistics Honours student in 1978. In the meantime he became the Superintendent of our hostel, First Mess (now KK Handique hostel). Later on when I became a lecturer of the same department, I became one of the closest students of sir. Though, he was an extremely good student and good teacher of statistics, I shall always remember him as one of the management Gurus of my life.

In 1979, I was appointed as Monitor of the hostel by Sir after getting an affirmative answer from me on his simple question, 'Are you ready to take the responsibility of a Monitor?' However, I was little bit upset after hearing from one of my classmates that offer was made to him before it was offered to me. I did not ask sir why my friend was offered the post before me till I became an ISS officer in 1985. He smiled and answered, 'I knew from the very beginning that you were far better candidate than him for the post of Monitor of the hostel, but I offered him before you to test his attitude of taking responsibilities. In the first one year, I have noticed each one of you and I found that he was always critical of others' activities. You perhaps noticed; he had never criticized you as a monitor during the whole tenure of your monitorship. Monitor's duty is to maintain free-flow of communication between the students and the Superintendent.' I did not know whether I was a good monitor or not, but I learnt a lesson, how to tame a disgruntled subordinate working under me as a senior officer.

In our hostel days, though now it may be ridiculous to be heard, we were not allowed to take chicken in our hostel. So one day as an expression of revolt, all of us forced one of the cooks to prepare chicken outside the kitchen and all of us relished the chicken curry. As expected, the matter was reported to Baruah sir by the cook and Baruah sir called me to his office room. What he told me for the next few minutes that became a great lesson for me. 'Hiranya, when the matter was reported to me, I thought some rogue boarders have done this. But when I was informed that you were also involved, I was not angry, but shell shocked. In one way you are agreeing that you are taking a bad decision by not cooking the chicken curry inside the kitchen and at the same time by forcing to serve the curry in the dining hall. Even if you want to revolt against a system, you should be sure what you want and what is your line of actions.' I took a cue from his admonishment and I alongwith other boarders met the Principal, Dr. G C Deka sir and included chicken in our hostel menu.

In 1981, sir scolded one the boarders at the top of his voice, when on the previous night in an inebriated condition, the boarder said something loudly very personal about sir. The student apologized and went on to become a very good doctor after few years of that incident. This was an eye opener for me, 'One has to take head on any rogue element to maintain discipline in any organization.'

As a Superintendent of the hostel, he always behaved like a true father. He made a communication channel, like our fathers in good old days used to do, through our mothers; through our respected baidew (madam), Smt. Dr. Hiranmoyee Baruah who herself was a teacher in Pragjyotishpur College of Guwahati. What we did not dare to communicate with sir, we easily told to madam. Even some of our ridiculous demands were met by sir when the same was communicated through our madam. Through that I learnt from him, few important things of life/ management. 'Always keep all communication channels to run an organization smoothly. Keep a distance with the subordinates, but always ready to hear their demands and needs.'

As a subordinate, I understood the importance of wife's view of my boss. Most of us will agree; we seldom dare to refuse a request of our better halves, no matter how unreasonable those are!

Jishnu Dutta Sir was a brother par excellence, he was a teacher any student could aspire for, a dotting husband and was an ideal father for his two sons. Probably, he was a student, any teacher in the world could boast of.

He was one of the sincerest sirs; I had come across in my life. For sir, students were the members of his extended family. Mrs. Dutta madam was a perfect folly of Dutta sir reminding the students of Guru and Gurumata saga of Indian mythology.

In a small town, Doomdooma of Tinsukia district of Assam, Dutta sir was born to a middle class family on first February, 1940. After his schooling, he joined Assam's premier college, Cotton College, Guwahati as a student of Statistics Department. At that time, nobody had imagined this lanky boy would be one of the finest teachers of the subject for thousands of students in due course of time.

He passed out as a master degree holder from Guwahati University in 1962 and joined immediately as a lecturer in St. Anthony College, Shillong, the capital town of the then undivided Assam (later on, after bifurcation of Assam, Shillong became the capital town of Meghalaya). It is worth mentioning that Shillong is known as the Scotland of the East. He spent in this beautiful city for two years. Then he was offered a post in Cotton College where he spent his fruitful 34 years of teaching life till he retired as the Dean of the Department of Statistics on 1st February, 1998.

But being a very devoted teacher, he could not sit at home for long even after his retirement. He joined Assam Institute of Management in the capacity of Controller of Examination in 2000 and continued there till 2002. However, his health started deteriorating since then and therefore; thereafter he associated himself in delivering lectures on honorary basis in different institutes instead of joining any regular assignment in any other institute.

Putting every student and his family members into a pool of sadness, he left for heavenly abode on 29th November, 2016 at a hospital, in Bangalore after suffering from a prolonged illness. He left behind his wife and two sons and their families along with thousands of mourning students speechless.

He married to Sumitra Dutta, a very dignified and beautiful lady. The couple was blessed with two extremely brilliant sons. The second son Anupam had a unique record of being topper both in Class X examination and Class twelve examination conducted by Board of Secondary Education, Assam. So far, none other than Anupam from Assam has achieved that enviable distinction. However, Bipin Borah, a classmate of mine, achieved this distinction with a curtailed manner (1976 and 1978, Higher Secondary where very few good students used to appear that examination in those days).

Apratim was also an extremely brilliant boy. But people see the comparative pictures only; and therefore, one has to agree, Anupam had been more brilliant than Apratim. What Dutta sir said about them? 'Apratim is more studious than Anupam. But Anupam has more receptive capacity.'

At the time of death of sir, both of his sons were married. Apratim settled at Bangalore with his wife Paulomi and their children Abhinav and Tanishi. Last few years, Dutta sir was living with Apratim and his family.

Anupam was living in USA with his wife Anwesha and daughter Aanya at that time.

However, Dutta sir had an extended family in his brother and his sister-in-law for major part of his life since brother had developed some medical problem. He had to look after his brother's family both physically and financially almost throughout his life without any complain. Rather, he was giving more comfort to his brother's family than his own. Only a very few great men in this world can do that.

For me, who was Dutta sir and for him, who was I?

Let us start with our last conversations before I was transferred from Guwahati to Delhi. 'Hiranya, you are becoming less shameless nowadays! Why?'

'May be due to my age, sir I am becoming less shameless.' I quipped with a grin. He smiled back with that innocent smile which all of his students wanted to see in his face. Why he asked me that question?

On that day, I said an unconventional 'No' for tea to Baideu (madam/ elder sister). Baideu and sir used to give me tea and snacks whenever, I used to visit them since 1976 as a Pre-University student.

I might be one of the few students who could boast to exchange light talks with sir. I was one of the most privileged students who were given the liberty to ask a few questions, of course not during my student life (1976-81).

During one of my visits to his home at professor colony, Cotton College, I asked him, 'Sir I know, I had never been one of the 'most favoured students' of you. But do you like me sir?'

With his trademark smile he countered the same question to me. I immediately answered, 'I did not like you and my own mother because of (both of you) yours over serious approach to life. But without iota of doubt, I love you as my teacher and my mentor.'

‘Probably, that is the reason why I love you also. You are never serious to your life. You never tried to achieve anything using your full potential. But still I love you.’ Sir thoughtfully told me.

I had told to my friends and acquaintances may be thousand times why I am here today. It was a silly morning of January, 1981 when I was taking sunbath, a classmate of mine from economics honours passed a message from Dutta sir in a bitter coated capsule. As per his version, he asked Dutta sir, how many students from statistics department would be able to secure first class in the B.Sc (H) final. On his question, Dutta sir mentioned few names. The list of probable first class holders did not figure the name of mine. When my friend asked him why the name of mine did not figure in the list, his answer was very candid.

‘How he will get first class? Has he any time for his studies? He is doing all the sundry works other than the work he is supposed to do. He has saddened me by his activities!’ At that time, being the Editor of Cotton College magazine, ‘Cottonian’, I was involved in many activities which were detrimental for excelling in my studies.

Those few sentences carried by the friend of mine from my respected Dutta sir, galvanized my attitude towards my studies. Unfortunately, at that time, only three months were left for the B. Sc final examination.

Few years later when I referred about the bitter pill he had sent through my friend, Dutta sir said, ‘Is it? Still I am not happy with you. You could have achieved much more than what you have achieved today.’ Sir told me with his usual seriousness.

As I grew older, sir sometimes treated me as a friend of him also. Sometimes he allowed me to discuss on some lighter topics as well. Believe it or not, sometimes he used to indulge some leg-pulling also with me. In one such occasion he poked me, ‘Do you know---? He was a very good student of mine. He wanted someone from Government of India to deliver a lecture on NSSO. He knows that you are in NSSO. But I told him not to invite you. I told him to invite some serious officer for delivering the lecture.’ With a twinkle in his eyes he finished his version.

As expected, I got the invitation to deliver the lecture on Dutta sir’s recommendation to the professor of Guwahati University.

So far, my relationship with Dutta sir is concerned, it was based on truthfulness on the part of Sir (no, I was always not truthful to him; but I always tried to be). Sir was always candid in his reply to any of the queries raised by me on general studies, on statistics or on social life. One day, when I asked him according to him among the intelligent students where I stood, his answer was frank:

'I have met many more students who happened to be more intelligent than you. Some of them are holding very good positions. However, some could not excel in their professional lives. That is a part of life.'

His opinions are always revered to me.

But what was the most touching statement he had made for me? Obviously, not those statements whatever had already been mentioned above.

A few years back, I confronted sir, 'I am not your best student; I have not achieved anything what many of your favourite students have already achieved; then why you are tolerating my nonsense for hours when we met after few months or so?'

'You will get the answer when your son will be in the hostel, away from you, knowing that he was not the most intelligent boy in the world, not the most handsome boy in the world, not the best achiever in the world, but still you will be waiting for him to hear his nonsense!'

Probably that explanation of sir summarizes my relation with Dutta sir. I always missed sir as a true mentor for a boy who came to Cotton college from a small non-descript village of Assam with a dream in his eyes to make something big.

I am extremely happy that both of his sons are extremely successful in their professional life. I always pray to God, Baideu will be able to withstand the loss of sir and will have a healthy and peaceful life without sir.

Now let me share something about Prof. (Dr.) Jyoti Prasad Medhi, popularly known as Medhi sir who was one of doyen of statistical fraternity of entire country and one of the most popular statisticians of the world. He was one of the pioneers of stochastic process in India. As a student of statistics, I know how much respected he was among the students and teachers of statistics in India. Due to my official position, I was blessed to travel all over the world to attend few official and un-official meetings and seminars on official statistics. In most of the places, the participants were aware of three Indian statisticians: Professor Mahalonobis, Professor. Rao and Professor Medhi, if not more than these three statisticians were known to most of the participants of all the statistical conferences I had attended across the globe. That was the stature of Medhi sir in the eyes of the statisticians' world over.

I was very fortunate to be able to interact with this mega star of statistics due to my friendship with his elder son Debu (Dr. Deepankar Medhi) and was also equally unfortunate not to be a student of Medhi sir.

At personal level, I was indebted to sir on many accounts. Prof. Medhi was referee on all of the applications of mine for higher studies and for jobs during my student cum un-employed days.

During 1979-81, I had to stay at Medhi sir's residential quarter at Jalukbari many times due to thrust-upon holidays by the college authority. During my stay at his residence at Jalukbari, I seldom opened my mouth before sir fearing he might ask me something on statistics. As a student of statistics, I had never been a student who had the audacity to interact with sir. Perhaps he also understood the mental condition of mine as soon as I used to appear before sir. Prof. Medhi sir always asked me questions on many things except statistics. I used to give answers in one or two words only. Debu used to tease me for keeping my mouth shut before sir being an over talkative boy in those days.

But when questions of career building of mine came to his court, he helped me like a true guardian. He advised me how to appear before an interview board, what should be studied for competitive examinations etc. Even when I and

Debu reached Delhi for our masters, he took personal interest so that we were not sent back by Delhi University for not having our result out at the time of admission. It is because of his personal intervention, I and few of my friends were able to get admission in Delhi University and in most probably without that help, I would not have been here, where I am at this juncture of my life.

When I was selected for Indian Statistical Service in 1985, I went to his residence (Debu was in USA at that time) to tell him about my selection, he hugged me like a father which I will not be able to forget till my death. That was the last time; I met Prof. Medhi at his University quarters at Jalukbari. After that, when I was posted at Guwahati as Regional Head of NSSO, I used to invite Medhi sir to inaugurate our training programmes to motivate the field officers and officials. In most of the times he was gracious enough to honour our invitations. During my stay at Guwahati I was a regular visitor at his Silpukhuri residence.

I learnt from him what modesty was. I learnt from him, how to bring up children to become good citizens not only for the country but also as the citizen of the world. I learnt from him how to motivate students/ children for higher studies without uttering a single sentence to study further, how to motivate an elderly person to work even after retirement. I learnt from him how to motivate a subordinate to work beyond his/ her potential without using a single harsh word. He motivated me how to live a disciplined life. He motivated me, how to beat diabetes to live a long and extremely fruitful life (He was diagnosed diabetes at an early age of 23 and went on to live a fruitful and active life upto the age of 93.) I was sure he had motivated many of his students and colleagues through his actions, not by words.

His demise few years ago created a void in the statistical fraternity which will probably never been filled in near future. But in the opinion of mine, his loss will not be limited to the statistical fraternity only; it is a great loss for the state of Assam as he was the only professional known in any professional discipline outside the country.

I was surprised to see how Sir was active till his last days at the age of 90 plus.

I am very glad to let you know that, his sons and daughters are well placed in the society which many successful people cannot boast of. As a friend, I am also proud of the exploits of Deepankar in the academic world and his career progression in USA in the last three decades. His brother and two sisters are also doing their best in their own fields. I wish all of them all the best for their future.

For me Prof. Medhi was a living God till his death at a ripe age of 93 at Guwahati few years ago.

Now let me tell you about my relation with another professor of statistics, Prof. Sudhendu Biswas:

I was closed to only one Delhi University teacher and he was my respected teacher, Prof. Sudhendu Biswas.

Sir taught me, how to bounce back in one's life after a massive set back in life. As I have already mentioned compared to all other results, I did a very bad result in my masters. I was devastated and thought that was the end of my career. I did not know, 'what to do' and 'how can I make a comeback.' I found myself at a state of depression and at a cross road. I did not know how to put the pieces together to start my career building once again from scratch.

During those turmoil days, I was blessed by the Almighty to provide me a glimpse of hope; I was able to snatch the last seat of M. Phil in Delhi University. There were only ten seats for the M. Phil course in those days and the tenth seat was offered to me. Prof. Biswas sir was kind enough to guide me in my research though I was the worst student on the basis of M. Sc final result. As all of you might be aware that in M.Phil course in those days there were two components of evaluation. First part was evaluated through written examination and the second component was evaluated on the basis of the dissertation submitted by the student and his performance in the viva-voce. Sir told me to forget about my M. Sc result and concentrate in my research on my topic: Multivariate modelling in Bio-Medical Science. Thanks to Sir's inspiring words, I was the second student of my batch to submit the dissertation and complete my M. Phil degree out of ten research scholars with high first class within a year. Further in the same year I was able to clear my UPSC examination on my very first attempt.

In all practical purposes, I could bounce back to do a far better result in M. Phil than expected by many and went on to crack UPSC in my first attempt to become an ISS officer only because of constant encouragement of Biswas sir.

Even after passing out of the M. Phil degree, he was instrumental in preparing for my career building. Though I had regular contact with sir, I could not meet him in his last days due to some unforeseen official assignments of mine during those days.

His son and daughter are already settled in their life. However, madam had left her family for her heavenly abode much before sir had left this world for his heavenly abode.

Those were the teachers of mine who taught me different lessons of life and they were teachers by profession. However, there were many teachers in my life who were not teachers by profession. They were coming from different professions of life. Among them I always remember one senior officer who taught me how to make official drafts for official letters. Another senior officer taught me how to manage large national and international events and another senior officer taught me how to write an official report. I shall remain grateful to these seniors as my gurus (teachers).

I have learnt many good things from my neighbours and relatives also whom I always consider as my real Gurus in my life. I am always indebted to them for their teachings to solve some of real problems that I had faced at different junctures of my life.

No doubt, a number officers and people of the society tried their best to teach me how to ditch and backstab friends and colleagues for my own petty gains. Unfortunately, I could not learn that art of living so far. Should I mention their names? No, I shall not do that; because I do not want to make them immortal like Mahishasur or Duryadhan alongwith Maa Durga and Yudhistir.

I am also thankful to all my childhood friends who taught me how to swim and how to steal plums from others' orchard when my own parents were distributing same fruits to the people free of cost from our own orchard. I am also grateful to all of my childhood friends who taught me to tell a lie to the parents for a good cause.

I am also grateful to my teenage friends who introduced me to a new world of love and romance.

I am thankful to my college and university friends who taught me how to push the friends to the laps of the unsuspecting ladies to spoil their career. However, some of us had never been pushed by others as none had felt it was necessary for us.

I am thankful to all my senior colleagues who taught me how to blame the juniors for their own faults and how to take credits for all the good works those had been done by the juniors. Probably I could not be a master of that art in my entire service career.

I am thankful to all my subordinates who taught me how to write anonymous letters complaining against the boss only because the boss wanted those subordinates to come to the office in time or to do some official work.

I am thankful to my children who taught me how to father them.

Last but not the least, I am thankful to my wife who teaches me how to fight without a reason, how to justify something which is beyond justification and logic. She happens to be my most influential teacher in my life like any other wife to her husband in this world. How I can miss any of her lessons, when she teaches me how to submit my apology to her for a mistake committed by her and not by me.

Chapter V: Mine fields of Humiliation

My service life was a mine field of humiliations. First I was posted at Giridih, a remote district of Bihar at that time and it is a district of Jharkhand now. Though my rank in ISS examination did not deserve that posting as those below my rank got their choice of posting, the cadre controlling officers thought perhaps otherwise for the first Assamese ISS officer and posted the worst place of posting without perhaps any remorse in their minds for doing an unjust work. However many attributed my posting at Giridih as a fallout of my wife's hospitalization during my field training at Mysore who accompanied me during the training. Even though no senior did extend any help to me in my days of crisis, they have every right to annoy over my decision to take my pregnant wife alongwith me to the field training oblivious of the fact that under what circumstances I had to take her alongwith me for a long tour.

But now I think that I am lucky to have few postings at some of the toughest places of the country in the early part of my career which ninety percent of my service officers cannot claim to work in such tough places in their entire service life.

As already mentioned above, my first posting after completing training period, few months before completion of my probation, was at Giridih, a small town of Bihar (now the Giridih falls under the newly formed State, Jharkhand) which did not have even some of the basic facilities normally a town of any other state used to have during those days. Bihar had been a backward state in terms of economic condition of the mass people crippled with caste and religious divide for at least in the last hundred years. During my stay in that dusty and under-developed town, I came across a popular saying of the people of Giridih, 'There is no load-shedding of electricity in Giridih; because current (electricity) seldom comes. (*Giridih me current kabhi jati nahi, kiyuki current kabhi kabhi aa bhi jati hei*).' I also realized in my one year of stay in Giridih that, if there was continuous supply of electricity for five days, the residents including myself were anticipating that there was a realistic chance that there would not be any supply of electricity for the next fifteen days. However, people of Giridih were extremely helpful and the place was good for people of lower income group as the cost of living in that belt was comparatively lower than other parts of the country.

Actually the town was in the midst of Mica mines and therefore, despite of being a very small city or a town, branches of all the Nationalized Banks were available in the city to cater the needs of the exporters of mica when mica was exported to different foreign countries. However, as those countries stopped importing mica due to substitute of mica was found at a lower rate for their use, the city also lost its charm. During the pre-independence era, Giridih was also considered to be summer resort for many famous Bengali stalwarts including Dr. Jagdish Bose, the famous scientist and Prof. P. C. Mahalonobis, the Doyen of Indian Statistical System. However, when I was posted at Giridih it was nothing but a dead city as described above.

My wife and I slowly liked the place despite of lack of any modern facilities in the city, because of the helpful people, good quality of ground water, good quality of the sweets and low cost of living in the city. Rs. 5/- as tips to the man who used to bring gas cylinder made wonder in our life, as none of the residents used to give more than Rs. 2/- as tips to him; the gas carrying man used to ask every one week if my wife was in need of a gas cylinder despite of scarcity of gas cylinders in those days. All the fresh vegetables, most of the local seasonal fruits and variety of fishes were available at cheaper rates compared to Delhi and Guwahati. Unfortunately, during that one year, my wife suffered from jaundice and had to return to Guwahati for some time.

After few months of her return from Guwahati she was again on her family way. When she was five months' pregnant, I was transferred to Kohima, state capital of Nagaland, a hilly state of North Eastern part of India.

I was transferred to Kohima to open one regional office of NSSO, FOD for socio economic data collection in Nagaland and Manipur. Though Kohima was a state capital, the population of the town was less than 40,000 people according to 1981 census. At that time the state was in turmoil due to the heavy fighting between separatists' forces and Government of India. I had to stay there for more than one year and was able to establish the regional office with lot of agony at the official and personal level. The small capital town was one of the costliest place of India unlike Giridih, but similar to Giridih in terms of having civic facilities. Anyone can understand the plight of a young officer with one and half year old daughter and a pregnant wife when I was transferred to that small town. As I seldom got any real help from anyone in the case of delivery of our first child, initially we decided not to tell anyone about the pregnancy of my wife. But my wife told me, 'if something goes wrong, everyone will blame you only. Therefore, it is better to call my mom for one month.'

Though, during the birth of my son, my mother-in-law was with us, the real help came only from the nurses of the Naga Government Hospital. Naga nurses were the best nurses in India in those days according to me and my wife. We find them that they were not only good nurses for the patients but also excellent human being who were always ready to help the patients and the attendants. They were doing their duties not only with devotion but also with smiling faces unlike the nurses of 'so called main land India' who were infamous for their frowning faces. We were always thankful the ever smiling beautiful nurses of Naga Government Hospital for their help and nursing during her stay in the hospital for more than one month. I sincerely hope they are still maintaining those good qualities even today and still they occupy uncrowned title of 'the best nurses of India'.

We always remember the people from Nagaland as people with broad heart, smiling faces and helpful attitude despite of the hardship they were facing due to insurgency that plagued Nagaland much before the Independence of India. Many people outside Nagaland may not know that, Naga people were extremely courteous towards unknown females. When we were living in Kohima, we were told that a lady could move around the city in the midnight all alone wearing jewelry on her neck as she would not be attacked even by the extremists or by any of the Naga drunkards who used to loiter around the town till midnight. On the other hand, a male after dusk was not safe unless he was with a lady or a kid. I used to move on the streets of Kohima at any time after dusk with my wife or with my daughter on my arms. Probably, in the so called Mainland India, ladies were (are) not safe to be alone at night and a man would not be safe from the thugs if he would be with a kid or with a lady. I always praise Naga people for their respect for ladies and for their large heartedness towards an unknown person. Another aspect of the Naga Public Representatives was praiseworthy; they used to mingle with common people without any ego, which was (is) also missing in my own state Assam or any other state of so called 'Main Land India'.

Being the people of a backward state, some of the Naga people believed some rumours without verifying the truth, floated by a group of people with some vested interest. Here is only one interesting rumour which was told to me is narrated below.

According to the rumour, in many villages of Nagaland, the strongest man used to acquire the power to become a real tiger and used roam around the village after dusk to protect the villagers from the intruders. It might be a good move to protect the villagers from the enemies in the earlier days. But in the turbulent times of the area, this particular rumour was fanned out by the ultras to their own advantage to deter the movement of the common people after dusk.

I being an educated person could not believe the rumour and due to my inexperience I could not foresee the danger of disbelieving the rumour as well. I was almost fallen into the dragnets of a group of ultras for moving around from one place to another even after dusk; but saved by the Almighty. Details of fallout of my misunderstanding of the intrinsic meaning of the rumour, I have narrated as fictional story in another book.

However, the weather and climate of Kohima did not suit my wife being an asthma patient. Due to cloudy weather in the most part of the year, she could not maintain a good health that gave me lot of headache during our stay at Kohima. In fact, she was suffering from asthma attack many times during our stay at Kohima little over one year. I requested one of my sympathetic bosses, Late Shri Ramanathan Iyer to help me out of the problem on humanitarian ground.

Luckily when my son was ten month old, I got my transfer to Guwahati, the home town of my wife. My posting at Guwahati gave me an opportunity to peep into the mentality of some of my own people towards a senior officer of their own community. They welcomed me as the first local officer as head of the office. I was in that office in two stints, the first one from 1989 to 1994 and then from 1998 to 2003. My sweet and sour experiences in Guwahati can be judged on my experience in constructing my half completed house. When my wife was struggling for her life, real help actually came only from only a few subordinates though ninety percent of my subordinates visited the hospital to fulfill their obligation. However, I was thankful to all of them for their good wishes for my wife during her hospitalization. During my stay in Guwahati I understood that fight for survival was always an individual issue despite of being in the midst of relatives and friends. No doubt if someone is living in the midst of his friends, relatives and his own closed families, his peace of mind is guaranteed up to some extent.

Coming to my first posting at Guwahati after my transfer from Kohima, on face everyone welcomed me in the office but some of them tried their best to malign my image from the very first day. Why? Because of some historical reasons and due to some purely personal reasons, a group of officials started conspiring against me from the very first day of my posting at Guwahati.

Prior to my posting at Guwahati as RAD Assam, the officer who was posted at Guwahati, actually completely spoiled the office atmosphere. Every clerical staff was irregular in attending office and some of the officials had monopoly in some lucrative works of the office and those officials used to behave like some rogue elements. None of those officials used to come to office in time; to be frank none of the officials used to come before 11 AM and all of them used to leave before 5 PM when office hours were from 9-30 AM to 6-00 PM. I had a tough time to make those late comers to be punctual and to break the monopoly of few officials in the office. The disgruntled official tarnished my image beyond repair. In the second stint due to upgradation of the office, I had to work under a stupid arrogant officer from Delhi. He thought he was the representative of Delhi Sultanate who was sent to Guwahati to rule Assam. The seniors posted in Delhi supported me in front but in back, they instigated my arrogant boss to backstab me. As a result of that, I was transferred from Guwahati to Delhi when our elder daughter was in class eleven and our son was in class nine and he also spoiled my ACR without informing me as in those days except the adverse ACR, ACRs with average grading were not to be communicated to the concerned officer. The reviewing officer who was always behaved with me in a goody-goody manner upgraded my ACRs to the grade of 'Good' which was actually below the benchmark for promotions to the JS level. I was eventually lost three years to become a JS level officer compared to my other batch mates. After my transfer to Delhi, I had tough time for more than one year in maintaining two establishments, one at Guwahati and one at Delhi with my meager salary. But thanks to the Almighty, my children were settled in Delhi within a short time after my transfer and were doing well in their academics.

When I had settled in Delhi comfortably, the same shameless seniors who were instrumental in spoiling my career requested me to go back to Guwahati as office discipline had been in taters once I left the office at Guwahati. Within six months of my transfer from Guwahati, the arrogant senior was allegedly beaten up within the office by another junior officer of the same service. Then many of the seniors sitting in Delhi realized under what conditions I was working in that office with that senior. Therefore, I refused to take the sweet words of those seniors at their face value. Most of those seniors who had tried their best to spoil my life when they were in power, but had been retired long back, wanted to make amend of their relations with me afterwards. Though I am not sure whether they tried to amend their relation with me because of self-realization or because of out of frustration of not able to spoil my family life and social life, I have forgiven all of them. Similarly, I have forgiven those persons working under me and who tarnished my image only because I wanted to make them discipline. I have also forgiven those seniors whose ego was so big that they could not see reasons and tried to harm me all along when they were in helm of affairs. Most of the officials who tried their best to tarnish my image from behind are mostly retired; some have very contended life and some have tough life as per the wish of the Almighty. Who am I to pass judgment on my seniors and my juniors; after all I also cannot claim to be the best man the Almighty had ever created so far.

At Guwahati we could stay for almost thirteen years with a break of six months.

I served in four places and more than 10 offices with different capacities in the last 36+ years of my service career. To my credit, during this period I opened two new offices (regional office at Kohima and sub-regional office at Imphal which are now upgraded to be headed by Director and DDG level officer) and purchased two office buildings (Guwahati and at Dibrugarh) and eight flats for hostel facilities of a zonal training centre (at Guwahati).

Unfortunately, officially I did not get any credit for all these creditable jobs {I got average ACRs continuously for 4 years with recording only with a single word against all the entries 'Average' (seventeen times in all) from my boss. Those ACRs were upgraded to 'Good' grading for all the four years by my super boss and unfortunately, which was below bench mark for promotion. Those are the testimonies of my good works in those years (sick!)} and therefore as expectedly, one will not find my name on the plaque of any of the buildings as my boss posted at Guwahati and bosses in Delhi thought my name should not appear as I was from Assam or I was too junior to be put my name on the plaque. However, I have no regret for that as I always think those negotiations were done by me as a part of my official duties only and for those works I was paid my salary.

Again, I had been given recordable warnings twice for some of my mistakes as Regional Assistant Director and as Deputy Director. Unfortunately, in the similar cases, however, for other officers, even memorandums were not issued. I had been issued a charge sheet for hiring a firm on nomination basis. When everything was done at the behest of the seniors and everything was done in a transparent manner, why in the first place I was charge-sheeted?

Let me allow to share some watershed moments of my service life with you.

My first recordable warning I got when I was a RAD at Guwahati looking after additional works of Regional Office of Nagaland without any additional remuneration or any additional benefits. In all practical purpose, a Superintendent level officer was looking after day to day activities of the RO Kohima office. Though, I suggested the FOD Hqs to bring the allotted vehicle of Kohima to Guwahati till a new RAD joins there as I was informed by some of the officials, the local Superintendent was misusing the vehicle, the FOD Hqs turned down my suggestions and my specific complain about misuse of vehicle was closed without any enquiry. However, after his retirement a new Superintendent took over the RO and he found the condition of the vehicle in a very bad shape. During that time, the Director in Charge of FOD, had informed me verbally to repair the car so that he could use it on his visit to Imphal after one week. As a dutiful officer, I conveyed the message to the new Superintendent to repair the vehicle on urgent basis. The bill was of around Rs. 11,000/-whereas the financial power of RAD was Rs.5,000/-. After few correspondences, I was given a recordable warning. However, after few years, when my Delhiwalla boss spent much more than the financial power of HOD - without taking prior approval of the higher authority, even a memorandum was not served. So, 'you show me the face, I shall show you the rule' applies to me.

In the similar fashion another recordable warning was issued for the similar reason, when I tried to give some benefits to the local officers and officials working in the Regional Office, Guwahati.

As a fall out of 'Good ACRs' for few years, when out 127 Directors 94 Directors were promoted to Deputy Director General (DDG), I found myself in the list of 33 Directors who were not promoted to the post of DDG because of having ACRs below benchmarks. It was very painful and humiliating, to say the least. The most officers who were not promoted because of bad ACRs, the ACRs were written by the senior ISS officers. Why ISS officers were instrumental in destroying the careers of the officers from the same cadre? I tried to find out the answer on this issue.

ISS officers use to garner least importance and respect outside office compared to any other Central Government Organised Service. It is ranked 12th in the Organised Civil Services among the 12 Organised Services. It is like 12th position in shotput final competition where in the final only 12 competitors were allowed after the semifinal. It is no doubt a prestigious service considering out of 100 other services it is coming in the top 12. But it is the last ranked service starting with an 'I' (IAS, IPS, IFS and so on). So inferiority complex of the ISS officers is understandable.

How to ventilate the frustration of being the last 'I' service is a major concern of the ISS officers. The ISS officers are bulldozed by other service officers as IASS (Indian Ass Service) though technically they were carrying best of the brains of India. Normally the ISS officers were best students at the school level. For example, in both X and XII, I scored highest marks from our school amongst the first division holder in Class X examination. The next best boy in terms of the results became an engineer; the third one became a Veterinary Doctor, the fourth one became a Doctor, the fifth one an ACS officer, retired as a Deputy Commissioner and sixth one became a Junior Engineer. In the eyes of general public, the fifth one became the most successful person in the society in terms of money and power. Doctors and engineers also have lot of value in the eyes of general public. Probably in the eyes of general public, I have the least value in all the societies; despite I was holding the highest position in the hierarchy of Government Services among my all the classmates of our school. There lies the reason of frustration of the ISS officers in general.

If you have read the story of 'On Saying Please', how bad behaviour percolates downwards quickly, you will know the ill effects of 'ventilation of frustration' of the ISS officers on the juniors. I always see the frustration in the eyes of majority of the seniors and I observed them in bulldozing the juniors day and night. However, expectedly, degree of bulldozing may be different for different officers and I found few of those highly frustrated lots as my immediate or super boss. Thanks to their frustration or due to my inefficiency I might be the only officer in the entire fraternity who not only had got 'Average' ACR from a particular boss for four years continuously but also got only single word 'Average' assessment for seventeen parameters. My super boss was clever enough to avoid 'intimation to the aggrieved officer' and upgraded to 'Good' grading though it was also below benchmark for promotion to the grade of DDG. It was like while reexamining paper marks were increased to 27% from 4%, without giving the necessary pass marks of 30%. Thanks to the Almighty, the Supreme Court of India advised the Government to do away with ACR system and introduce a transparent system of assessment by the seniors (APAR) and I had started getting 'Outstanding (8/10)' Grading after introduction of the system. Except one occasion I got more than 9/10 grading in the last 10 assessments. You must be interested to know who gave me less that 9/10 grading in between; yes he happened to the best friend of my previous boss who gave continuously 'Average ACR' for four years.

You must be thinking I have lot of grudges against my seniors who gave me below benchmark ACRs. Yes, I was hurt and humiliated at that time. But today, I have nothing against them; rather I am very much thankful to them. Had they not given me below benchmark ACRs, I could have retired as a DG instead as a DDG. But had I got an above 'benchmark ACRs' all along, I would not have pursued my old hobby of writing stories, novels and poems. I do not know whether as a writer I am successful or a failure, but I have lot of satisfaction for being recognized as an 'Author' of many books and hundreds of ebooks. As one of my books was received by the Honourable PM Sir in his chamber at the Parliament of India and tweeted from his personal tweeter handle, I felt that I should be thankful to the Almighty for all my success than keeping bad feelings for those backstabbing seniors.

For any officer facing disciplinary proceedings is nothing but a huge embarrassment and public humiliations. I also got that and to humiliate more, even after IO gave a clean sheet to me in 2019, the cadre controlling office kept pending my case at their level so that they can humiliate me again and again. They left me high and dry for the last phase of my career and promoted those officers who were few years junior to me. But I am one of those shameless officers who neither committed suicide nor had suffered a heart attack so far.

Do you want to know the story of my agony of being charge sheeted in details?

In 2010 a contract was awarded to a computer firm to develop 'software' to enter village level data. As expected the State Government could not complete the stipulated task, and being the Director of the scheme, I proposed to extend the contract of conducting the training for the officials of the respective states and to provide technical support to the same firm in consultation with the seniors. After few up and down the file, the proposal was approved by the AS & FA of the Ministry. Subsequently, the first instalment was released. However, after one year when for the second instalment file was moved, the file was approved by the then AS & FA and the Secretary of the Ministry had approved the file for releasing the second instalment. However, when it went to the Director, Administration, he objected for release of the second instalment with the comment that while awarding the contract competitive bidding was not done and that is why the contract should be scrapped. On the advice of the Secretary, the contract had been scrapped.

As per the contract, the amount payable to the firm has been calculated. But they demanded a much higher amount which Government denied to pay. The firm went to the Delhi High Court where they lost the case. However, the moment the firm filed a case, as a knee jerk reaction, the Department charge sheeted me, my immediate boss and (it is hearsay) my super boss were charge sheeted for major penalty. As my super boss expired during that period, only my boss and I were charge sheeted on 31.12.2015, on the day my boss had been retired from the service. Later on the Director IFD was also charge sheeted. Incidentally, all the three officers from ISS cadre and those who also signed on the file at different level, but all the officers from other cadres were spared due to the reasons best known to the administration. As our ISS Association thought the case was an individual one they preferred to remain mum and we three had to face the music.

Then our ordeal started. The first IO preferred not call even for a single hearing, retired on 31.10.2016. The second IO took almost two years to hear few witnesses but did not submit any report. Finally 3rd IO completed all the formalities of the enquiry on 31.05.2019 and submitted his report in the month of August. We all the accused officer are thankful that IO for obvious reason. But the Disciplinary Authority issued another memorandum asking some clarification on completely new points. The reply on the new points was submitted by me in time and long lull has been observed by all the lesser mortals since then till April, 2021. Finally, the Director IFD was awarded a minor punishment before his retirement on 31.07.2021 for not following GFR properly; but they did not question the role of the AS & FA who was an IAS officer. Similarly, just before three months of my retirement I was also awarded minor punishment without any financial effect on my retirement benefits. I am thankful to the UPSC and DA (Disciplinary Authority) for closing the case before my retirement and of course the Almighty for showing them the right path.

I knew it was inevitable. But when I was left out again and again from the promotion list from DDG to ADG, I felt humiliated again and again. Throughout my ordeal, few officers from my own cadre and other cadres, few of my friends and my family stood by me for which I shall remain grateful to all of them.

Many people think that I had been an unlucky mascot for my bosses. Some people are complaining about my unlucky status, because five of my bosses expired before their retirement, two had died within a very short time after their retirement, one was arrested by CBI for allegedly taking bribe from his subordinate to improve his Annual Confidential Report, one of my bosses had been allegedly beaten up by a very junior officer in his own chamber with chappal and one boss had been charge-sheeted alongwith me. Conveniently, both of the above two bosses, as expected blamed me for their ordeal. However, most bizarre thing happened to one of my bosses few years ago. The foreign visit of that particular officer was cancelled citing that a CBI case had been filed against him for misappropriation of public money. The humiliated officer was later on informed that, actually case had been filed against another officer from another service who had the same name. It was a case of mistaken identity for having the same name. Therefore, it may be said, the accusation against me might have some truth. But the fact of the matter is that many of my bosses have attained the highest post and still they are hale and hearty even after decades of retirement. Whether there was any truth on my unlucky mascot tag or not, one powerful senior officer did not dare to join in his new place of posting as my boss and he had joined in that division only after I was transferred out of that division.

Further all my bosses who have died at relatively at young ages and who suffered some major to minor humiliations in their life, had their own un-enviable stories to tell to their peers and therefore I do not want to share those stories in details with my readers honouring their dignity before my esteemed readers. This a small description of my service life with some good things and bad things, but no doubt a long one with full of romance and uncertainty.

Some of my extraordinary achievements as Government servant are shown in the annexure in the form of some office orders, citation etc.

Again, I want to analyse why I am not a very good officers in the eyes of some of my bosses. I am sure most of my bosses will not agree my analysis for the obvious reasons. Whatever, may be their comments on my analysis, I am sharing my analysis with my own perspective only with you.

In a sense I was the first generation of Government servants in my family though my parents were also Government servants as teachers of Government and semi-government schools of Assam; because teachers are having complete different work culture and profile than a bureaucrats and technocrats of India. Therefore, after coming to the fold of senior bureaucrats (or technocrat?) as a direct recruit officer, I could not shake off the baggage of the son of a teacher in my style of functioning in my work places during my entire career. Though I have always been polite and hard working, I could not be a 'yes man' to some of the stupid and arrogant bosses and therefore I had to suffer a lot as a Government Servant. However, I was (am) not the only person who suffers from that uncompromising attitude.

During my long career as a senior Central Government officer I have been experiencing many ups and downs in my life. Many times, I faced lot of problems due to not handling of some of my inefficient and arrogant bosses properly. I never had any problems with the intelligent and hardworking bosses in my entire service career; I always took their advices and scolding as only blessings of teachers or my well-wishers. But whenever I had to work with bosses with lack of knowledge but with huge egos, I had lot of problems in working under those bosses. Everybody knows, most of the bosses are like that only and therefore, if I could not handle those inefficient bosses efficiently, that shows my inefficiency as well. Politics in work places are also not a new thing which will be elaborated here as many of my esteemed readers may know more than what I had experienced in my entire service career.

However some snipe shots from my long career make some funny and educative stories which are actually emanated from the bleeding heart of mine due to endless assault on my heart by particularly those who were in the helm of affairs in those days. Continuous bleeding in my heart was as a result of humiliation I had to face during my career primarily because of my rural background, inability to speak fluent English with jargons, my over protective nature for my juniors and due to inability to take credit for the work I had done and my inability to blame my juniors in front of my seniors for their fault. But here only some of the stories which had lot of influence in my personal life will be penned down which, however, might not be a part of my assigned duties.

What type of officer I was? From the day one, I was an unwanted person in this world so was in office. In the office also, no boss wants me in the first place. Let us generalize this problem faced by few unwanted persons in the societies around us and beyond.

All of us have to agree one thing without much argument that, in this world some persons are unwanted and not liked by most of the people and on the other hand, some are always wanted and always liked by majority of the people. Expectations from the wanted persons are different from the unwanted persons by the societies, offices, bosses and subordinates. In an ideal condition, expectations from the wanted persons should be more than from an unwanted person. But in reality, it may be opposite also; not necessarily always. Particularly in offices, bosses expect more output from the unwanted persons but he will never be liked by his bosses.

However, in any society, liking, expectations from wanted and unwanted persons may have high positive correlation because it evolves over the years. On the other hand, relation between subordinates and boss evolves for few days to maximum for few years only. Life is very short and therefore, if a person was informed directly or indirectly by the other person that he/ she is not a wanted person in his/her life, both the parties should act fast to improve the situation if there is a scope for improvement or otherwise they should take a conscious decision to take their own ways with a promise not meet again in this life.

Take the same question once again; what will be his/ her reaction, if a person was informed directly or indirectly by another person that he/ she is not a wanted person by him/her? He/ she will think he/ she must have some deficiencies; which other person has noticed in him/her or other person has some prior negative feedback from other sources. If you are the person who is unwanted by someone, in such a situation you have two immediate alternatives, leave the place and never show your face to the person in your life or try to convince him that you are not a bad guy or an inefficient guy or a man of deficiency what the other fellow has been thinking about you. But for the second alternative, the other fellow must give you a chance to explain your position. But seldom have we got the required chance in our lives.

Let us discuss the specific case of mine. I experienced the feeling of unwantedness, on most of my transfers from one office to another. At every new office I used to get some unwelcome signal from top to bottom, might be true for everyone on anyone's transfer. But every time, after six months in the office, I became an integral part of the office discussions and official works only because of my hard works. After few years of associations, even many of my immediate bosses were reluctant to release me on my transfer citing my transfer would create a void in the office. In fact, as a result of my indispensable status in Delhi in one office I had to serve almost 13 years in different capacities; as Joint Director, Director and Deputy Director General. However, I did not see anything great in that long innings as during that period I was denied promotion for three years and one charge sheet was slapped on me which lingered for more than six years with a decision of imposing a punishment of downgrading two increments for few months resulting few thousand rupees. But due to prolong indecisiveness on the part of Disciplinary Authority cost me two promotions also as a result of which I had to retire as DDG instead of DG from the Government.

In the next office in Delhi, I was almost to be thrown out of the office in the first month itself. But I remained in that office for more than five years till my retirement. In fact, in Delhi from 2003 to 2022, I got only one transfer. Then why I was not welcome in a new office?

I tried to decipher the strange situation for my own good, but I am yet to solve the puzzle without further scope for discussion. Is it because of my 'not so attractive face' or due to some negative body language in the eyes of the seniors? Or some negative feed backs given to the new boss by some vested interest parties? Is it because of my rural background? Is it because I am not fluent in English? Is it because I always pass on the credit to my juniors and take all the blames for any failure unlike other bosses who claim all credits for all the good works and blame the juniors for every failure? I am still clueless about that. But fact of the matter is that initially always I had to bear the brunt which used to hurt me emotionally in the early part of my career. Am I an unhappy man in the long run? In the initial years of service, I felt very bad about those situations of neglect in the new office and sometimes I even became depressed which affected my peace of mind in the family front as well. Luckily for me and my family, as I grew older, I sometimes started enjoying those situations; rather later on, I started loving the tag of an unwanted person. Later on I became very confident that within six months, I would be able to gain the confidence of my bosses and my subordinates.

A few years back one intern from a reputed university told at the time of completion of her internship that she was very much disappointed to meet me on her first day due to my rustic talks. But after two months of her association with me, she realized, she would have missed a gem of a person had she not worked with me. However, her sweet talks may not reflect the true picture of mine; after all she was in need of an excellent certificate for her internship. If however, her interactions with me after one week and opening up her heart to discuss some personal problems with me to solve those problems are any indications, then perhaps she was truthful to her comment on me.

I also agree, being from a rural background, I have some genuine problems of 'desi ascent' which most of the English medium educated people ridicule in the first one or two months of their associations with me. Unlike other people, the truthful intern admitted that she ridiculed my English in my absence in the first week with her fellow interns. But after one or two weeks, each of the interns might have realized my knowledge on some of the subjects and therefore I was able to earn some respect after every discussion on few of the subjects I have discussed with them.

I feel that if I was not wanted somewhere initially, it need not necessarily mean that I had some shortcomings except my inability of speaking English fluently which may be the most essential qualification to survive in the midst of the elitists of India and South Asian Colonies of British Raj. Being a statistician, I collected some information regarding direct recruit officers of Government of India, recruited before 1990 and found more than 90 percent have urban background whereas even in 2011 census urban population of India was less than 31% which was much below than 20% in 1991 census. In other words, probability of being recruited in a good job for an urban youth was 36 times more than a rural youth during my selection to the job by UPSC. So my selection to the elite class of Government of India in 1985 was not a small achievement considering a lopsided selection process in India; am I boasting?

I cite one example (not necessarily true for me) for many people's unwelcome move for a particular dashing person; 'Suppose that particular person was not invited to a party, because the host did not want that all the young ladies would be after that particular fellow, whereas the host was going to foot the bill. Suppose, fortunately, or unfortunately, knowingly or unknowingly, that particular person gate crashed into the uninvited party, how the host would welcome the gate crashing dashing person? That is simply impossible for a normal human being.'

However, my somewhat problem solving capacity might be the actual threat to my inefficient bosses in front of their respective bosses. That attracts all the hostilities towards me from those clueless bosses and colleagues working in the same office contributing nothing to the system for years together.

My take away from long service career where I had to report to bosses with intelligence and lack of intelligence is: useless and less intelligent bosses are mostly carrying big egos and therefore they cannot convince his/her subordinates through logical/ technical debates and tries to bulldoze his/her juniors through official position. As a result of that condition, there will be bound to have frictions between the senior and the juniors. Since as a matter of convention or rule of the law, the hopeless senior is protected by the system and as a result of that the junior suffers without any fault of his/ her.

Despite of having so many obstacles in my service life, I have been informed by a reliable source that I am going to get the scale of an Additional Director General (Additional Secretary Rank, I was drawing the scale of a Joint

Secretary before my retirement) from back date at the last leg of my career because of the blessings of the Almighty, Mother Goddess and faith of some very intelligent seniors in me throughout my career.

Chapter VI: Other Than Service Life

No one in Guwahati thought that I had been selected by UPSC while I was in Guwahati looking at my standard of living, intelligence level and so on. If I go by the misinformation campaign by my juniors in the office and the perceptions created by the seniors, I should have maintained a high profile luxurious life. But it was completely opposite so far my life style was concerned during those days for which my neighbours thought I was a clerk in a subordinate office. Once, a shopkeeper refused to believe that I was a Deputy Director in SSC as I was driving a scooter to purchase my gas stove. Similarly, an owner of a furniture shop laughed at me because I ordered only four chairs for my dining table and refused to buy the claim that I was an officer selected by UPSC. A young representative of a drug company hailed from Bihar also aired similar view on my job.

Nevertheless, I was known as a very corrupt man in the eyes of my seniors posted in New Delhi and perhaps they are keeping the same view which was diametrically opposite to the views on me by my neighbours and relatives, particularly in the eyes of my in laws family.

Another, impression many of neighbours and friends from the so called upper castes has been carried out even today, as I belonged to the Ahom Community who had been declared long back as an OBC category, I got my present job due to reservation. Just for information, reservation in central government for OBC category started in 1992 onwards and I was selected for all the jobs, including this one in 1985. Further, I would like to clarify that not only me and any of core my family members had never taken any reservation of Government, both state and central. Because, though I cannot change my caste, I am ashamed to admit one fact in my life: being a ruling class of Assam for 600 years uninterrupted, why we could not forgo this benefit for the sake of self-respect?

Therefore I had never taken any benefit of being OBC in my entire life and did not allow my children also to take any benefit of being in the OBC category.

However, still I support reservation policy of Government of India because it is not only needed for economic reasons but also for social reasons. I feel reservation should be abolished when the persons who are coming up at par with the persons with the unreserved persons both in economic and social parameters. An engineer's son may not need reservations looking at his father's economic status. But what's about his social status? Even with all the constitutional protections, he or she may have to face social boycott from the so called upper caste people in social functions. Unconstitutional reservations are more dangerous than constitutional reservations and unfortunately that not only does exist in the society/ offices but also followed with immunity and with rampant misuses. Before abolishing the reservation policy, in my opinion all the upper caste people will have to forgo their surnames which clearly mentions about the caste of the people. In other words, we have to leave aside our surnames first and then only we can think of a casteless society which will lead to a society free from all reservation policies of Government. There is an old saying, if you point a finger to others, four fingers of yours are pointing towards you. I am sure; my reply will not be liked by most of the people from unreserved category having surnames flaunting their superior caste and creed. Even I felt very bad when my son could not get a seat in a reputed engineering college in a stream which he opted for and on the other hand when one of my colleagues' son who got it with at least 10,000 rank below my son's rank. However, when I heard the trauma of the boy in class IX and XII despite being a son of a senior officer, I was appalled and I thought actually he should get a reservation when we are yet to give same launching platform to all of them.

A lady classmate of mine had humiliated me with many strong words as a writer when she was requested to review my book, 'Blessed One'. She used her choicest words to demean every part of my book so that I would not dare to write a book again in English in my life time. She, being from a so called from the upper caste, though her results in the class had never justified her superior caste, teared into my social status and rural background for my poor English and as a selfish man of 'all time.'

Luckily for me in the very next month, Honourable Prime Minister of India, my most beloved political leader, Shri Damodardas Narendra Modiji invited me to his chamber at Parliament Building to receive my next book, 'Chandraprabha: The Iron Lady of Assam'. After receiving the book he also tweeted about the book from his personal tweeter handle. In that book, how caste system prevailing in those days spoiled the life of Chandrapraha Saikiani, I had showcased. The Hon'ble PM Sir told me in no uncertain terms that I should write on the unsung heroes and heroines of India. I became so inspired by his words that I was able to write, 'Mula Gabharu: A story of Valour and Patriotism' within three months after getting his invaluable advices.

Chapter VII: Mis-Information Campaign

If you were from my service, senior to me and if you were posted in Delhi or in Kolkata you might have been aware of the palace constructed by me when I was posted at Guwahati from 1989 to 2003. The persons posted at NSSO (FOD) also knew about the magnificent palace constructed by me during that period. Many of them swear by the name of God to see the palace of mine at the heart of Guwahati city. For the magnificent palace, I had been referred by those who were aware of the palace and opulence of mine nicknamed me as the 'King of Assam'. I used to enjoy all the nonsense spread about me from those seniors and some juniors closed to those seniors. There was a group of seniors who in front of me congratulated for every achievement of my children, but they were planning to disrupt my family life so that my children would not be in a position to achieve anything in their life. However, I am thankful the Almighty for His divine interventions all along in my life so far and all the three children of mine are settled economically and established themselves in their professional life, perhaps they are better placed than 95% of Indians by the grace of God.

The myth of having lot of money and having a large palatial building was created by some of my subordinates of a particular group posted in the Regional Office at Guwahati and some officers posted at Kolkata and Delhi due to some vested interests in doing so. Though I knew why the subordinates were doing that (due to some historical reasons) and due to inherent disliking for people from North Eastern Part of the country of some seniors sitting in Delhi, I damn cared for those as I had full faith in the justice system at the Court of the Almighty and therefore I never lost my sleep or lost my smile and laugh even when they ganged up to destroy me continuously for more than few decades. Believe it or not; one senior officer once admitted that my ACR was downgraded only because he thought I was from reserved ST category of Assam. According to him, he was little bit confused with my surname 'Borah' with 'Boro/ Bodo'. Of course many juniors also thought me from ST category as I hailed from Assam. Anyway these might be some aberration only for some of the officers.

Coming to the construction of the palatial building that had been constructed by me at Guwahati, the readers may be interested to know the facts behind such a fuss. In reality, I tried to construct a house on a plot given by my father in law which was purchased by father in law in 1963, to my wife after six years of our marriage, on persistent advice from my father in law to construct a house. However, once house construction had started, I realized that I had committed the first major mistake in my life.

With a family of four, having only a single income, construction of a house became a 'Bhalukar Sangi (carrying a live bear / riding on a tiger) for me. I got thousand advices from thousands of people on construction of my house, but none was ready to pay a single rupee to tide over my financial hardship. I withdrew almost every rupee from my GPF account and took a loan from a private bank. I took some personal loans also from my friends and colleagues. To save the amount on rent, I had to shift my family to the incomplete house even without basic facilities, like electricity and water, just to save the bill on the monthly rents. After the shifting of my family, I got the electricity connection after three months and got water connection after six months. My family, particularly my first two children being children of a Group A- officer of Government of India even could not get proper meals on regular basis during those days. But some of my colleagues (who actually never helped) floated a rumour that I constructed a two storied palatial building with my corrupt money. I was emotionally drained, but I was helplessly looked around for some help, but I got neither any financial support nor emotional support from anyone.

In between I was transferred to Delhi in the same capacity (probably I was transferred being a corrupt officer to teach me a lesson) for the fourth time as most of my senior colleagues knew that I had constructed a two storied palatial building with carpet area 2500 Sq.ft in each floor). However, I got a deputation posting at Guwahati after six months and was able to stay in Guwahati for another eight years; exactly three years in that deputation post; though the borrowing department wanted to keep me for a longer period but my cadre controlling authority thought otherwise and posted me on promotion at the same office from where I was unceremoniously transferred three and half years back.

As soon as I joined the old office, my palatial building also became bigger and bigger on every passing day as per the two groups who were fanning the rumour of constructing the palatial building few years back. Finally, when I left for Delhi on my transfer in the same capacity (the authority did not wait for my next promotion which I got just within three days of reaching Delhi), the ground floor of the building with less than 1000 sq ft carpet area was an incomplete house (which otherwise in Delhi, most of my senior colleagues knew that I had a two storied palatial building with carpet area 2500 Sq.ft in each floor when I was transferred to Delhi eight years ago).

I was aghast when after I had settled in Delhi properly (both the elder children were studying in their respective degree colleges situated in Delhi), same group of senior officers who were instrumental in transferring me when my daughter was appearing for XII final and my son was appearing for Class X final Board examination, offered me a post at Guwahati on humanitarian ground (sic). However, I thanked all those great people for showing their large heartedness in offering me a posting at Guwahati to help me and my family. I thanked the Almighty to send these people to my life for making me stronger and might be more successful beyond official life.

With that bad experience I never thought to buy any flat etc. in Delhi or in NCR (National Capital Region). However, as luck would have it, after Sixth Pay Commission, I got a good amount as arrear and my elder children had already joined in multinational companies after completing their studies, therefore I was able to book a flat at Faridabad with an estimated total cost of 35 Lakh. I took a loan of Rs. 25 Lakh from the same private bank once again. But the builder took nine years to hand over the flat against the promised handing over time of three years. Finally when I got the possession of the flat in 2018, I had to pay little less than Rs.50 Lakh.

Even to book a flat in the NCR, I was forced by a comment from a relative of my wife, before my son when he had visited Guwahati in 2007 as a student of an engineering college of Delhi. A guest of the relative asked my son, 'Where you are going to settle after your father retires? Have you purchased a house or a flat in Delhi?'

Before my son could reply, the relative sarcastically replied, 'Oh, they have to come back to Guwahati. His father has constructed a small house on a plot donated by his father in law to his wife.'

After returning to Delhi, my son told me about the comment made by the relative. That comment triggered me to buy the flat located at Faridabad.

While looking back, I think I did a good job by constructing the building for the following main reasons: a) the experience of constructing a house gave me an opportunity to know about the people close to me. b) One should not take any decision as per the advice of any relative including the in laws. c) One should not believe about the promised helps from anyone as all are likely to back out at the right time leaving you high and dry. d) If you belong to a middle class family and become relatively more successful compared to your other relatives, never expect any help from anyone even when you are in dire need of financial assistance (including while constructing a house or even when someone from your core family is in a hospital fighting for his / her life) from any of your relatives.

The other index of opulence is: a person having a vehicle or not at a particular point of time. Therefore let me share with the readers about my scooters and my cars.

I bought my first scooter (the first automobile I had bought) in 1992 after completing six years of my service. Why my first scooter is mentioned as the first automobile purchased by me? Actually when I was posted at Giridih, I purchased a bicycle to go to different places including to the office despite criticism of the lower rung officials of the office for downgrading the status of a Group-A officer in the eyes of the common people. But I ignored their criticism and visited many places of Giridih with that bicycle so long I was posted at Giridih.

My first scooter was a Narmada Prince which was launched in the market only one year prior to my purchase. I purchased the Narmada Prince scooter for its height and for its relatively less price compared to popular Brand during that time, Bajaj Scooter. The scooter served me and my family for almost nine years till I purchased my first car in 2001. I used to take my family from one corner of the city to the other corner of the city on my two wheeler; initially, comfortably and as the children grew older, with lot of difficulty.

Since, in Assam and may be in other states also, a Direct Group A Officer riding on a scooter was a rare view, many people thought me as a Group C or at best a Group B officer of Government of India. As already mentioned earlier, when one day when I went to buy a gas stove at Fancy Bazar of Guwahati, the shop owner refused to agree that I was the Deputy Director that too at Regional Office, Staff Selection Commission (a place where black money was flowing like water of Brahmaputra which was a public perception for the common people in Assam). I had a tough time to make him understand that without corrupt money (pre-sixth pay commission era) a Direct Recruit Group-A Officer cannot afford more than a scooter in the first ten years of service, unless he gets a car from his in laws as dowry.

Whatever, general public thought about my status, I used to enjoy the scooter riding with my children at least during Durga Puja time. We used to visit one puja mandap to another puja mandap without much difficulty in negotiating with Guwahati traffic in Puja time.

She (the scooter) gave me her best service when my wife was in hospital for 54 days fighting for her life. The scooter provided me the best possible help by carrying me on her back from one pharmacy to another pharmacy in search of medicines. For a rare life saving medicine, methyl prednisolone, I had to cover entire Guwahati in three days. Doctor prescribed for eight injections and since the injection was very costly (Rs.840/- per injection and my monthly salary was merely Rs.7600/- as a Deputy Director in Government of India during those days), no pharmacy used to keep more than one injection at a time. With all my efforts, I could manage six injections only with prescribed 1000 mg of methyl prednisolone. For the rest of the injections, I purchased 4 injections with 500 mg methyl prednisolone. The medicine had huge side effects and to neutralize the side effects, the attending doctor prescribed another 17 medicines for which also I had to travel the entire city on her back. For taking a lunch or for taking a dinner also she carried me one dingy restaurant to another posh restaurant during those trying times of my life.

My first scooter served me and my family more than any relative and more than any friend in my life, perhaps.

My first car was a Maruti 800 white car. She was with my family for more than eighteen years, giving us best possible services. Before disposing her, I bought another white car, Honda Amaze. Finally when she was wheeled out by a Maruti executive, she was replaced by another small Maruti car as a tribute to the white beauty.

I shall be always thankful to her in rest of my life for giving so much happiness in my life for more than eighteen long years through her services.

In my eyes, she was extremely beautiful with her dazzling white marble colour when I bought her in 2001 when I was posted in Guwahati as a Deputy Director at NSSO Regional Office. However, like all others cars in Guwahati, she had also been painted black on the bottom side to prevent rusting due to red muddy water of Guwahati city.

I still remember vividly my first long journey by my new Maruti car from Guwahati to North Lakhimpur, a sleepy city of eastern part of Assam just after seven days of her purchase, against the will of my family members. All my family members were very much concerned about the security and safety of both of us; new driver with a new car. Bowing to my adamant nature, they agreed to my proposal to visit North Lakhimpur by my new car.

Being a new driver with a brand new car, I took special care that neither of us should get too tired to go up to North Lakhimpur on a single day. First, I took rest at Tezpur which is 180 KM from Guwahati. Tezpur was the district HQs of my hometown. Tezpur had been a favourite destination for me, not because it was my district HQs, but because this was the home town of my most favourite Aunt who expired in 2002 just after her retirement. During that visit I decided not to visit her residence while going to North Lakhimpur; but to visit her home while coming back. So I took rest in a roadside restaurant for one hour while taking my breakfast.

When I reached my destination, it was 7 PM and darkness had already descended in the city. After taking dinner I went to bed; despite I was damn tired, at every hour I got up from my sleep to see my car. It was a full moon night and as moonlight fell on her body; her beauty was enhanced, at least in my eyes. Was I madly in love with her on that night? Cannot be said for sure; but still I remember vividly that full moon night.

Nowadays recalling those early days with her, I am feeling sad about her. She had been with us since 2001 March till 2019 and she had been a true companion of me for more than eighteen years.

When I bought the car in 2001, my salary was about Rs. 22000/- PM ($1100/- pm) and car costs him R.236, 000/- which was about 11 months' salary. Out of the total amount of Rs.2,36,000/, an amount of Rs.117, 500/-was taken as a car loan from government and the rest amount was arranged from my personal savings, savings at my wife's account and loans from my near and dear ones including my mother in law. I had to compromise the colour of the car; originally I booked a car having Safire blue colour, but had to settle for the car with milky white colour to save Rs. 3,600/-. I also could not install music system at the time of her purchase due to financial crunch. Therefore, I promised my children to install a music system after few months, which I could not keep during the entire period of her stay with us.

Finally, when I bought the car after almost sixteen years of my service, I felt like Duke of Wellington who had defeated Napoleon Bonaparte in the war of Waterloo. However, the wife of one of my neighbours had doused the flame of winning a war, by her comment: 'Nowadays, anybody can buy a car by taking loan from bank.' (Incidentally she is the wife a person whose service was much below in rank compared to my rank.) Till today, my wife taunts me for the comment of the lady. Till today my wife reminds me how I had spoiled our first fifteen years' of married life by not buying a car. She still tells our younger daughter, how we used to travel on our scooter on rainy days. Therefore, due to purchasing of my first car, many things had been changed in my life from that day. From 2001, irrespective of rains or sunlight, my family was able to go to a cinema hall or to a picnic spot. All my family members had a feeling of new empowerment after purchasing of our first car in March, 2001.

Though, I had a valid driving licence much before I had purchased the car, I had little experience of driving a car. On the fourth day of purchasing the car, I made a freak accident while putting her inside my newly constructed garage. In the said freak accident one of the head lights was broken and one of the doors was dented. In the process, I had to cough up Rs.4000/-on repairing the brand new car. All my relatives admonished me for my careless attitude. But that did not deter me from driving my car and after one month, I became comfortable in driving the car. I undertook my first long journey with the car just after a week which has already been shared with you above.

Just after one month I drove her to Nalbari, a small town, 65 KM away from Guwahati. This journey will always be a memorable journey for me because I realized for the first time that one intelligent police officer could be more effective than 100 ordinary policemen.

Those who have visited Guwahati know that north of Guwahati has been connected by one rail-road bridge, named after famous battle of Saraighat over the Mighty Brahmaputra and during that period of time, it was a narrow two lane bridge. For those who are not from Assam or adjacent areas, for them it is a mere bridge only, but for Assam and Assamese people, the bridge symbolizes valour of Assamese navy and army of seventeenth century. In a decisive battle, Assamese army under the leadership of Great Ahom General, Lachit Borphukan defeated Imperial Army of Mughals led by Rajput King Ram Singh and pushed the Imperial Mughal Army out of Assam border.

The rail- road bridge was opened in 1962 for public and considering the traffic in 1962, it was quite wide to accommodate the traffic during that period. Thanks to exponential traffic growth in India in the last few decades, the bridge became, like many other bridges of India, overburdened with traffic congestions during the period when I had to cross the mighty river driving my new car in April, 2001 to make field inspection in a village of Nalbari District.

When I reached the bridge at around 8 AM I saw a huge traffic jam on the bridge. On enquiry I came to know that, a mother elephant was killed by a bus in the early morning when she was crossing the bridge along with her three month old cub. The driver alongwith three other passengers also lost their lives in the accident. It was not known why the baby elephant started running on the bridge. But once the mother elephant saw her cub was running, she also started running defying the orders of the Mahout. The driver of the bus, coming from the opposite direction could not control the bus and collided with the large animal. The impact of the collision was so huge that the elephant died instantly. Along with the driver, three passengers also died instantly leaving few other passengers seriously injured. The bus halted at the railing of the bridge obstructing vehicular movements on the bridge.

When I reached the spot around 8 O'clock in the morning, there were already thousands of stranded vehicles lining up to cross the bridge from the both sides. There were at least one hundred police men standing helplessly without taking any action to remove the dead body of the elephant and the ill-fated bus from the bridge. They could not find any headway to clear the traffic jam. One of the police officer suggested to push the elephant to the river which was objected by other policemen considering the religious sentiment attached with an elephant in the North Eastern part of India.

At around, 9 AM, the Additional SP of Kamrup district arrived at the scene. He inspected the scene and then with the help of the police personnel present there, pulled the vehicle from the railing and put the vehicle along the bridge. Then he, again with the help of police personnel, pushed the elephant to the same side of the bus. By doing so, he was able to clear one side of the bridge, which was enough to allow movement of the traffic taking the other part/ side of the bridge. Then he controlled the traffic by allowing one side of the traffic move slowly. Luckily for me, my side of the traffic was allowed to move first.

Unfortunately, after three months of that incident, while controlling traffic before Rajiv Bhawan, Christian Basti, Guwahati, that police officer was hit by an unruly vehicle and that brave officer succumbed to his injuries after fighting for his life for few days of the accident.

The car had never given me any real trouble in her long association of more than eighteen years with me. That includes my long journey with the car from Guwahati to Delhi in 2004 without any major trouble except a puncture of a tyre near Shahjahanbad after covering almost 1850 KM out of total 1950 KMs to reach Delhi.

On, 9th May, 2004, under the scorching hot and humid climate, I started my journey with my fifteen year old son from Guwahati to New

Delhi. Despite of resistance from many of my well-wishers, I took my son for the long journey from Guwahati to New Delhi as my only companion. My son appeared in the Class X final examination in that year. His presence made me more cautious and wary in my driving; but his company made me very happy throughout the journey. The car was completely full with household goods including our old B&W TV.

On the first day, we travelled from Guwahati to Kishangunj, a very small town of Bihar, without iota of trouble covering a distance of 556 KM. After travelling 556 KM in a single day, both of us were damn tired physically; but not mentally. On the next morning, we started our journey at 5 AM. There was a stretch of 20 KM near Koshi River, where practically there was no road on the ground. The small wheels of the car used to submerge completely in most of the gutters made by the trucks. But due to sturdiness of the car, we could reach Patna comfortably, covering around 390 KM on hot and humid climate, taking only 10 hours on that day. An officer of Bihar State Government who hailed from Patna expressed his surprise when I told him that I had covered the distance between Kishangunj to Patna in 10 hours.

He exclaimed, 'How you could come from Kishangunj to Patna within ten hours, sir?

Practically there was no road between Purnia and Barauni.'

I thanked the Almighty and my car for my almost 10 hours' smooth journey from Kishangunj to Patna with my teen aged son.

We stayed two nights at Patna and then we started our journey from Patna to New Delhi on the day when NDA (National Democratic Alliance) led by BJP (Bharatiya Janata Party) lost the general election to UPA (United Progressive Alliance) led by the All India Congress Party. Because of victory rallies in different constituencies we could not travel at a desired speed. Finally, we had to make our overnight stay at Fatehpuri after covering around 500 KM from Patna. The owner of the hotel was a nice Muslim gentleman who allowed my car to get inside their closed boundary for the night.

Throughout my journey from Guwahati to New Delhi, there was only one unscheduled stoppage; that was at Shahjahanbad, a small town of UP, due to puncture of one of the tyres. The puncture was also not due to the fault of the car; a stray nail struck into one of the tyres. Even after that unscheduled stop, we were able to cover around 530 KM on that day to reach our destination, Pragati Vihar Hostel at Lodhi Road, New Delhi.

My Maruti car was the only car in the office where I had been posted for around thirteen years from 2003 to 2016, which was used by each and every colleague of mine at least once in all the thirteen years of my posting in that particular office. Except in rare cases of one or two, the car did not give me any trouble while I had ferried my colleagues from one office to another office.

There were many colleagues, after entering into the car gave unsolicited advices to change my car because of the model and because of the facilities in the car (without AC in summer particularly). Though I understand; it is a human nature to aspire for better life; somehow I liked my car from the core of my heart and therefore I did want to change the car initially even though the car started developing snags one after another on monthly basis.

In fact, she had never ditched me and my family while driving at night or when I had to go through some dangerous patch of the city. By the grace of God, she did not meet any major accident in her entire period of eighteen years of her association with me. What else I can expect from her? That is why I did not want to discard her, even after I purchased my second car. The second car has all the modern inbuilt facilities. But so long the first Maruti car was with me, while driving the car; I always felt a sense of peace of mind.

My son and younger daughter learnt driving and were able to take their driving licences with that car only.

However, due to the scarcity of space to keep three cars in front of my residence, I had to exchange my first Maruti 800 with a Maruti Alto 800 in 2019 with a heavy heart.

Forgetting the first lover by a person is extremely difficult in his/ her lifetime; for me also it will be very difficult to forget my first car in the rest of my life. Probably that was true for each member of my family also.

Chapter VIII: Shoes With Wings

We inherit many traits from our parents, irrespective of the fact whether we like those or we do not like those at all. I am no exception. Liking for travelling, probably I have inherited from my mother. I had seen, even with limited resources, she had travelled more places than my father, who perhaps did not like travelling at all. Now, I hope to pass on the instinct to the veins of my offspring even though my wife likes to stay at home more than travelling outside, even though she also claims otherwise.

I have already visited 35 out of 37 States and Union Territories of India; the two UTs, viz. Ladakh, and Lakshadweep, I am yet to visit are very small in size. Most of the State capitals of the large states have been visited more than once and a few have been visited more than even ten times by me. Even after 10 visits to those capital cities, I am always looking forward for another visit to know something more about that city.

Two habits of mine may be in my forte: one- addressing a public meeting/ students for hours and two- hunger to travel and making friends from all sorts of life. I always try to observe all the things around me minutely as far as possible on every visit to a city though I cannot claim to be a keen observer of life. I have both good and bad experiences while travelling around the country and around the globe. But I always use to share, as far as possible, only my good experiences with my friends. However, for a fair comparison between two cities or amongst the cities I have already visited, I try to mention some comparative aspects of different cities with others.

During the long and eventful married life of mine with my wife, spanning over more than three decades, we have visited many Indian cities or places of tourists' interests. As a couple, we have visited almost all the state capitals and almost all the major cities of the country in the last three decades. We have experienced many memorable incidents in those cities to tell our grandchildren, if we are blessed to have. Experiences of visiting some of those cities are shared in an ebook 'Shoes with Wings'.

However, I always travelled to the foreign countries on official tours only and therefore unfortunately (because one has to face all the problems likely to come up in an unknown country all alone) or fortunately (one can enjoy his/ her travel without any string pulling by his/ her spouse and without carrying other's baggage) my wife could not accompany any of those tours I had made in the last twenty years. However, she travelled to USA with our younger daughter to meet our son once in 2016 and stayed more than one month with him which might be more than total days of my stay in 10 foreign countries/ cities till that day. My foreign visits have also been shared in the same book, 'Shoes with Wings'.

The following foreign cities I have visited so far:

Melbourne and Sydney (Australia)

Vienna, (Austria)

Thimphu (Bhutan)

Beijing, Guangzhou, Hongkong (China)

Seoul, Daejeon, Incheon (South Korea)

Kualalampur (Malaysia)

Manila (Philippines)

Bangkok (Thailand)

Washington D.C., New york (USA)

For details please go to this link:
https://www.smashwords.com/books/view/1134256

Chapter IX: The Foodie

I have a heavy body fitted into a frame with a height of 5`10`. I should have a maximum weight of 78 KG as per BMI circulated by many health magazines. However, my weight hovers around 95 KG which shows that I am a 'over weight' person. But as all of us know that over weight is a disease which is side effect of our life styles. Among many other reasons, food habit also plays a pivotal role in making a person with a big belly. I am also no exception. I am sure; my belly will not be an 'envy' for anyone in this world. Every year, I am adding few cms in my belly without much thought over the years for a steady increase of my already over sized body.

Being a foodie, I wrote an ebook, 'Akhadya', published by Smashwords, on different experiences of having (or getting) different types of food under different situations in the last few decades. However, since the ebook was written in 2015, the book needs a complete overhauling. But still my esteemed readers may like to read the book and therefore, I am sharing the link of the book below:

https://www.smashwords.com/books/view/59
3664

Chapter X: The Incorrigible Writer

I am an incorrigible writer for many of the readers around the world including for my family members and for my close friends. Even then I write at a speed at which normally even a reader does not read his favourite books. In a span of eight years I have written more than two hundred eBooks and fourteen printed books. It may be a mystery for many, what drives me to write so many books in such a small span of time with such a hurricane speed. Am I a very popular writer? Have I written an eternal book? Have I written a classic? Do I write very good and perfect English? Do my books contain high degree of literary value? You can put any question against my writing skill; but you will get only one answer, 'no'. My books might have lot of spelling mistakes, full of grammatical mistakes and might not have been smooth and free flow to read. Then naturally a question will be coming to anybody's mind, why I write in the first place and for whom?

Writing for me means a way for ventilating my emotions and imaginations. I want to let others know what I think and what philosophy guided me to follow my life. Many may ask me; if my books are not read by anyone in this world, what is the use to write books? My counter question to them was; what is the use to read a 'good book'? We never follow the good advices given in those books; but those books are read by millions of readers. Actually, while a reader reads for his own satisfaction, I write something for my own satisfaction, like a reasonable customer who buys something as per his/ her own satisfaction and consumption, not for the satisfaction of the seller of the goods which may include a book also. Many people made good library by spending lot of his/ her hard earned money for his/ her own satisfaction; only to get rid of the library by his/ her son after his/ her death to make proper (?) use of the space. Even sometimes to make sitting space, office libraries are dismantled by the concerned authorities. There are people who have habit of gardening; are they going to earn anything out of that or are they going to be world famous? There are many people who are involved in painting knowing fully well that they cannot surpass the glory of Picasso or Leonardo Da Vinci. Then what is wrong if I spend money and time in writing some incorrigible books for my own satisfaction. Yes, there is a very good reason to criticise me for executing my habit of writing incorrigible books; paintings are rarely in public domain and very few people have the knowledge of looking at a painting in a proper perspective; while reading a book or keeping busy in gardening is a personal affair and on the other hand once your book hits a book-self many people can go through it and a book can easily be understood by a common man. There is another reason for criticising a writer for his incorrigible writings, people think, books are the reflection of the societies and any ill-informed book may likely to mislead a society. Moreover, every writer (for that matter every human being) is having a hunger for praise and that leads to a pain in the heart of a writer. Therefore, if any ruthless criticism hurts me also as a normal person or as a writer; but so far their criticism could not stop my writing habit and style of writing so far, no doubt I had left writing for many years in between 1980 to 2013 on personal ground.

I started my writing in my mother tongue, Assamese when I was admitted to the high school as a student of class IV and I got the first taste of public humiliation at the decision of the school authority to send me to sit with the ordinary students as I did not come to the school with the tag of a student who appeared for scholarship examination. I wrote a poem on that night to ventilate my emotions. The first recognition came as a writer to me when I was able to get a third prize in story writing competition in class VI. My first story came in an Assamese periodical, Bismoy when I appeared in my tenth final examination. Slowly I became a regular writer in some other periodicals as well.

But my serious writings on Assam agitation took an ugly turn and stopped writing on any subject for a pretty long time. My marriage to my wife and subsequently bogging down with family responsibilities, financial crunch etc. were also dampener for developing my writing skills. There was a lull of my creative writings for the next thirty odd years though during that time as I was involved in writing guide books and official reports, my skill of writing has not been rusted totally. In the meantime, due to my official duties, my teaching skills and skill of delivering lectures in public gathering have improved a lot. Finally, from 2013, I started writing unrelated stories in a hurricane speed after encountering a small incident with a senior which is narrated below.

There was an important publication of a particular department; the publication was however becoming heavier and heavier on every passing year due to addition of data sets on every successive year to the publication without deleting the old irrelevant data sets. A lady officer was entrusted to take the responsibility of the publication for the issue pertaining to the year 2013. She was reporting to me and one day she came to me with a suggestion, 'Sir, the publication looks to be a heavy one with important data and statistics; but unfortunately it is heavy only in look and weight, not in substance.'

'Tell me your plan.' I asked her plan of action as I knew that the lady officer was a very sincere officer in her works.

'I want to make major surgery to get rid of the unnecessary flab of the publication.' She submitted.

'Ok go ahead.' I gave her a 'go ahead' without thinking much on the issue as I had lot of confidence in her ability.

In the next one month, she had virtually re-written the whole publication and deleted all the unnecessary tables and useless data. The publication became leaner and meaner from 350 pages to mere a mere 125 odd page government document of substance. I had written the preface on behalf of the highest authority of the department as usual. When the file was submitted to the officer next to the highest authority, first he tried to admonish the lady officer for making the report so lean and thin. But as I was also present there I took on him, 'sir both, the file and the report have come through me and I have already approved both of them.

So I am fully responsible for whatever in the file and the report.'

'Borah you are always suffering for this habit only. Always you support the juniors and fight with the seniors.' He scolded me without showing any mercy on me for the next few minutes. Old habits die hardly and therefore, I also retaliated.

'Yes sir, you are right. That might be my worst weakness in my service life. But I do not care for that weakness; rather I am always proud of that habit. Even if I am going to lose many things for this particular habit as an officer, I am not going to change my approach at the fag end of my career. I am sorry sir. ' I laughed as if I was rubbing salt on the bruised ego of the boss.

Before the boss could comment or admonish on my reply once again, the highest authority who had to give the final approval called the boss alongwith me and the lady officer to his room to discuss on the report by his intercom.

Looking at the report, the highest authority looked at the lady officer and told, 'yes, you did the right thing by making the report lean and thin instead of making the report unnecessary voluminous.' Then he read line by line the preface and changed only one word of the draft preface and signed on the draft preface and approved the file.

Two days after publication of the report, a leading National News Paper quoted different statistics alongwith the preface as the version of the highest authority. I congratulated the lady officer for her good work and she also praised me for the preface which was quoted as said by the highest authority as his version on the overall situation of the country on the subject matter. All the persons who were even remotely involved in the report were called by me to my room and had a cup of tea with all of them and I thanked all of them for their excellent team work led by the lady officer.

After a week I got the opportunity to meet my boss and told him, 'sir, a good review has come in '–' newspaper on our report. Have you seen it sir?'

'Yes, I have seen it. In fact, I am getting at least 50 calls every day for the last one week from different persons congratulating me for the nice report we have prepared.' The boss boasted.

His boasting for the report, where his contribution was nothing but a negative comment, infuriated me so much so that, I vowed to myself silently, 'In the rest of my career, I shall write only for me, on my name and shall contribute minimum to any report where my boss and the super boss will have the last say and will have all the credits without doing anything and will be passing every shortcoming/ criticism to the shoulders of the subordinates.'

That was the starting point of restarting my creative writing.

However, I had to pay for my audacity to defend my junior before the boss; that particular boss made a point not to send me to any foreign country to represent the department as he thought I was not a good officer who only used to defend his juniors without contributing to the system. However, I had no regret for defending the junior in front of that Boss and losing a few foreign tours.

But why I was in such a hurry to write so many books without giving much time to see that spelling mistakes and grammatical mistakes do not occur? My argument is on that, spelling mistakes and grammatical mistakes can be corrected by any Tom & Jerry if I spend a few thousand rupees, but ideas and thoughts only I can give as and when those would come to my head and heart during the day or at the middle of a night. Feelings and creations are more important than writing few correct sentences on a subject like writing a government report with almost 100% correct English. All of us know that those reports are not read by anyone except the ruling and opposition parties of the Government to support or to say something against the Government or make few parliament questions.

During the last few years, I have written lot of eBooks, some of which are widely read across the globe and some were trashed to the dustbins by esteemed readers. Luckily for me, not even 1% of my friends and colleagues have the time and intention to look at the garbage produced by me as a writer. Less than 1% of my friends and colleagues who showed tremendous courage to read at least one of my books, I am always grateful to them for their love for me. Recently one of my friends asked me, 'I saw one of the recent eBooks published by you have more than 400 likes on your facebook. You must be minting gold from your books.'

'Yes, you are right. I am earning few bucks from the sales of my books; but not from those friends who liked the news on the facebook that a new book has been uploaded in the eBook platform or when the hard copies of a particular book have been launched. Even my friends, colleagues, and relatives are not downloading the free books. Why then they will download a book written by me by paying the price of the book, that too in dollars? Most of my friends and relatives claim that they know before opening the book what has been written in the book and they also know without even reading the first page of any of my books that the standard of the book has been so low that the book does not deserve a look into it.' I replied with a smile.

'Are they not downloading even free books? Then why you give the news on the facebook that you have uploaded a new book?' My friend demanded to know.

'I usually give the news of uploading of a book for receiving good wishes and blessings from the well-wishers. In fact, none of the relatives, friends, and colleagues usually read a book of a relative, friend and colleague as they think, what he/ she is going to write (garbage only) as a book is already known to them. This is not only true for my books but also true for all the books. In my case, my friends give best wishes and also give wide publicity that I become a writer. Further, I am not a professional writer, I write for my own satisfaction. Writing a book is like giving birth of a child by a mother. The labour pain of each mother is almost same with almost all the other mothers across the globe while delivering a baby; but only a child of a lucky mother will be a great person after some time. Similarly, every writer writes with his or her best of abilities, but only a few are able to write good books. That is the tragedy or beauty of life. One must accept both praise and brickbats as the blessings of the Almighty: for a writer, the Almighty is represented by the esteemed readers. They are the real masters to make you or break you as a writer; not by the critics.' I stopped there.

As my friend kept mum, I asked him, 'have you read any of my books so far?'

He meekly replied, 'no.'

I as usual gave my villainous laugh to the utter discomfort of my friend and then of course I consoled him, 'do not be upset my friend, other friends are also not reading my books. But if possible, bless me to write something which may be useful for at least one person out of 6 Billion people of the world. A renowned writer once told me, if a book is read by five persons in this world, your effort is successful as a writer. I know, except few small time writers like me, none will agree to his encouraging words. But we believe him and that is why we are yet to stop writing.' I heaved a sigh.

My friend did not say anything and left my place leaving behind the complimentary copy of my latest book; might be intentionally.

(List of my books and ebooks are given at the end of the book.)

Chapter XI: Association with SBM and JJM

15th August is one of the most important days for each and every Indian of Independent India. After 1947 till 2014, 15th August became a day of performing a ritual where Prime Minister of India delivers a lecture from the podium of Red Fort giving a list of policies of the Government India which were to be implemented in the next year or in the next few years. In fact, unfortunately nobody takes those policy declarations very seriously including the implementing authorities and agencies of the Central Government and State Governments. Had it been taken seriously by the implementing agencies of the Governments, India would have been a super power by the end of the last century. Because of this attitude of the Government agencies over the years, Indian people also became habituated to think that the lecture delivered by the Prime Minister is a list of 'what should be done for the nation' but definitely not a list of 'to be implemented by the Government'. Therefore, it became a ritual to be conducted by all the parties only to be forgotten till announcement of another set of policy formulations on the next year's Independence Day. All the important agencies of the Government were asked to prepare a list of 'should be done for the nation' using excellent catchy English which should be translated into Hindi for the PMs of Hindi Belt or otherwise may be kept as it was.

All the suave PMs of India till that epoch making lecture on 15th August, 2014 of the present Hon'ble PM, used to talk on some issues normally 90% of the Indian population could not understand what he or she was speaking about except something on 'Jai Jawan-Jai Kisan' and 'Garibi Hatao.' As a result of that, the Prime Minister's twenty point programmes formulated in the seventies crossed more than forty years without much progress. So nothing was expected from the New Prime Minister also on 15th August, 2014 by the common people of India. But on that day Hon'ble PM, Shri Narendra Damodardas Modi stunned not only the suave Indians but also the entire world by saying something which 90% Indians could easily understand and felt they got a PM from among themselves; hitherto all the PMs except two were from a different planet, many common people thought in that way only.

To substantiate my argument let us go through the list of Prime Ministers who served the country since our independence in 1947.

There were two exceptional PMs till Modiji was elected as the PM of India in 2014. Out of two, one was from NDA, Late Atal Bihari Bajpayee. He had served our country for six years. He was a son of a primary school teacher and he will be remembered by the Indians for his unprecedented push for infrastructure development in India.

The other one was, Late Lal Bahadur Shastri who served the country for merely 1.5 years who was a son of a poor farmer. He pressed for upliftment of lives of Kisan who toil their day to feed the nation and the soldiers who are fighting at the border. He evolved the slogan, Jai Jawan-Jai Kisan (Hail the farmers-hail the soldiers).

Now look at the list of the other PMs of India.

Our first Prime Minister, Pt. Jawaharlal Nehru (17 years) was the son of Pt Motilal Nehru, who was reportedly the first Indian to import a car for personal use. Though Guljarilal Nanda became two times interim Prime Minister of India, normally most of the Indian people do not consider him as a Prime Minister of India. The third Prime Minister, Smt. Indira Gandhi was the political heir and daughter of the first Prime Minister of India, Pt. Nehru. After emergency, Late Morarjee Desai became the Prime Minister of India for 2.5 years who was also from a very rich businessmen family of Gujarat. The Prime Ministers of less than one year period, Late Choudhury Charan Singh (19 days, extremely rich farmer of Western UP), Late V. P. Singh (11 months, known as Raja Sahab, king of a princely state), Late Chandra Sekhar (five months, Bhondse Baba of Balia), Deve Gowda (11 months, an extremely rich farmer of Karnataka), Late Inder Kumar Gujaral (10 months, son of a Cabinet Minister of Nehru Cabinet), all were from rich families. Similarly, the rest of the Prime Ministers, viz. Rajeev Gandhi (5 years, son of Smti. Indira Gandhi and grandson of Pt. Nehru), Narasimha Rao (5 years, extremely rich person of undivided Andhra Pradesh) and Shri Manmohan Singh (10 years, an Oxford/ Cambridge illumine) were also from aristocrat families of India. Undoubtedly, the post of Prime Minister of India has been occupied mostly from elite class of India, whose bathrooms cum toilets are costlier than the residential accommodations of 95% Indians. So they had never ever talked about the construction of toilets in public; probably they thought it was below the dignity of a Prime Minister of India to talk about construction of toilets in public, that too on Independence Day from the wall of the Red Fort.

On that day, Hon'ble Prime Minister, Modiji said something about the basic need of at least 50% of the total population of India, the women for maintaining their dignity by avoiding the humiliating experience of going to defecate in open on daily basis. He talked about providing toilets to all the poor households of India. Many people thought it was nothing but 'Election Jhumla'. But there was no election looming over India like earlier when a few 'Khisri (Coalition) Governments were formed during 1989 to 1991 and 1996 to 1998 without single party majority. With 283 BJP MPs in the Lok Sabha there was no threat to pull down the Modi Government by anyone. Then why he promised something which was apparently impossible to achieve? It might be because he saw from a close range how the ladies of his family including his own mother used to suffer mentally and physically for not having toilets in their premises or not even in their compounds.

In 2014, toilet coverage in rural India was barely 29% and to make it hundred percent coverage, India had to build at least 10 Crore toilets in rural India and around 3 crore toilets in the urban areas. So people of India particularly those who were sitting in the opposition or supporting the opposition by heart dismissed the promise of the PM as a non starter. However, most of the people from Gujarat were sure that he would be able to fulfil the promise of providing toilets to almost 10 Crore families across the country, no matter how tough it would be; because they know him as a Chief Minister of Gujarat for more than 12 years and they were sure; whatever he had promised in public, he used to deliver.

In the next four years what transformed in India was nothing short of a miracle and people of India declared themselves as Open defecation Free (ODF) on 2nd October, 2019. Though the Hon'ble PM is claiming that during this period, more than 10 Crore toilets were constructed without saying that it was 100% coverage or not. However, in many sense, the Hon'ble PM Modiji inspired the people of India to make a 'Mission Impossible' to a 'Mission Possible' (of constructing toilets in the tune of 10 Crores of toilets in mere 4 years time). How it was possible may be a case study for the whole world at present and it will be written in Indian History as the soft power of India under the leadership of a dynamic visionary leader in Shri Narendra Damodardas Modi who was taunted as 'Chaiwala (tea vendor)' only to be fit to distribute tea at Congress HQs by one of the prominent Congress leader during 2014 Parliamentary Election.

As per the mandate of the Government of India, the Ministry of Drinking Water and Sanitation was entrusted the duty of providing toilets in rural India through active support from the respective state governments. The Ministry was specifically instructed to complete the task by 2nd October, 2019 coinciding with the 150th Birth Anniversary of Mahatma Gandhi, Father of the Nation. To the satisfaction of all, for the first time in the history of India, a Mission (Swachh Bharat Mission) had been completed on or before the target time in all the States and UTs irrespective of political party in power in these states and UTs.

If you can complete an impossible mission in time, you are again likely to get a task which is also appeared to be an impossible task to be completed by a target date. Yes, the same Department (after 2019 the Ministry of Drinking Water and Sanitation has been merged with the Ministry of Water Resources and the name of the Ministry became Ministry of Jal Shakti) was given the responsibility to provide household tap connection of drinking water to all the households of rural India by 2024 December. This time none on this earth disbelieves the promise of our beloved Prime Minister, Narendra Moddiji. Though unfortunately Covid has made havoc in India alongwith other countries of the world, we are on the right path with reasonable progress in the last two years. And therefore, we are confident that we shall be able to complete the task of providing functional household tap water connection to all the households of India through this ambitious mission in time.

I humbly request to my esteemed readers not to be worried; this chapter will not be another government report of self-glorification nor self-glorification of some of the officers associated with the Mission. This chapter will help you to understand the feeling of common people of India about the change in their life due to availability of household toilets and functional household pipe water connection for drinking water through my eyes. I had been a privileged officer who was associated with these two missions. However, in the eyes of the persons who hogged the limelight, rightly or wrongly, I was in the Ministry/ Department without any significant role at all. Therefore, please rest assure; I shall not write a single sentence on my contribution to these two missions though I had joined this Ministry/ Department on 28.06.2016 when only one State, Sikkim and 6 districts out of 700 plus districts were declared themselves as ODF and household tap connection percentage was officially around 11% in rural India and when I left the Government on my retirement on 31.03.2022, the percentage of functional household connection was more than 50%.

From here onwards the real story of implementation of SBM and JJM will start.

After six-seven months of my forced resting time (most pleasant time of my entire career for which I will be remain grateful to my boss and the officer who briefed my boss about my inability to solve any problem and known for my inefficiency), I was sent to different states and Union Territories to reduce my fat already gathered around my oversized stomach during my leisure time with a fat free salary.

During a visit to a village of Assam, an eighty plus grandma caught my hand and told with a voice laced with satisfaction, 'my son, I thought I shall die without using a pucca toilet at my home, but Modi (as if the PM Minister of India is her own son) has given me a pucca toilet which I am using for the last one year. Convey my thanks to Modi.'

As if, I used to meet the Prime Minister on daily basis and as if, I was competent enough to convey any message to Hon'ble Prime Minister directly, I replied with lot of confidence in my voice to her, 'Okay, grandma I shall do it for you.' In a sense, I bluffed the old lady that I was so close to the Hon'ble PM of India that I was in position to convey any personal message to the highest authority. However, I was aware that during that period I was not the only bluff master in the Government or elsewhere. At least, in my department many will agree that one of my bosses had been a better bluff master than I who wanted to hoodwink everyone, from top to bottom with his often uttered claim before his subordinates that he was very close to PM and he used to claim that he only cared for the PM; not even to the powerful HM; forget about his other small fry bosses including some of the Cabinet Ministers. Now, one can understand who the real teacher of bluffing in my office was during that period.

Anyway as I was about to leave her compound, the eighty plus lady called me once again from behind, 'Please listen to me my son, you convey another message to Modi; I thought gas (gas connection for cooking) is only for the rich people of our neighbourhood. But before my death, I understand if the king is good, poor gets all the facilities from the government. Please convey that this old lady blesses him for his healthy long life so that poor also can live in this country with dignity and pride.'

Being not a privileged officer, as expectedly, I could not convey the message of the old lady of Morigaon District of Assam to the Hon'ble Prime Minister sir as per the wish of the old lady. However, I told that particular boss to convey the message of the old lady to the Honourable PM as he always claimed to be very close to the Honourable PM in those days. I was not able to know whether the message of the old lady of

Assam reached the Honourable PM, Modiji through my boss or not, but I am sure; the unadulterated blessings of the old lady reached the ears of the Almighty for the long, healthy and successful life of the beloved PM of our country with a multiplier effect, if getting a thumping majority in the general election of 2019 was an indication of the wish of the Almighty.

Similar experience, I got during one of my visits to a backward village of Meghalaya, another North Eastern State of India. A gentle man of around 70 who did not know English and Hindi, replied through the State Coordinator of the SBM scheme, 'I got all the benefits of the Modi schemes including a sanitary toilet.'

Through the State Coordinator, I wanted to know other than getting the incentive money for a toilet what are other benefits he got from different schemes launched by the central government during that period of time.

He gave a long list of schemes such as scheme through which he got a cooking gas connection, a residential house, household electricity connection, household piped water connection, health insurance coverage, Kisan Bima scheme and so on.

As expected even working in an office of a Ministry, I did not know that so many CSS (Central and State Sponsored) and CS

(Centrally Sponsored) Schemes were implemented during that time. I was surprised to know how the state government machineries were able to deliver the benefits to rural households in such far flung places of the country. I realized that Modi Government's success lies in bringing efficiency in the last mile delivery of the schemes. Otherwise, being in Government, I knew many of the schemes implemented under the Modi regime were introduced by the earlier governments also with different names, however, mostly in the memory of one family of the country without bothering about implementation of those schemes at the ground level. The earlier Governments, most probably were more interested to introduce the schemes only to make the names of that particular family more famous and immortal than implementation of those schemes at ground level to make India clean, rich and powerful with a bottom-up approach.

Coming to the old Khasi person, I found him not a novice like the Assamese old lady of Morigaon District and that is why, the old Khasi villager did not request me to convey any message to the Honourable PM nor did he send any blessings through me. Did I become unhappy realizing the depth of knowledge of the old Khasi fellow about the ongoing schemes and his assessment on my worthiness? Yes, perhaps. But, to be fair to me, in the eyes of the old Khasi villager also I could very easily see his gratefulness and unadulterated blessings for the Honourable Prime Minister.

Another reaction of common public from rural India rebutting the views of a group of people who portrayed through some anti-establishment media that the majority of rural people were not happy with the actions of the NDA Government, had floored me in September, 2018 in a backward village of Assam.

The Prime Minister of India, Shri Modiji decided to interact with few famous and ordinary common personalities across the country on 16th September, 2018 to impress upon the common people through those interactions that how much cleanliness is important for improvement the image of the country in the eyes of the people of the other countries, its importance in reducing medical bill of the poor people, employment opportunities, its importance for girl education and most importantly how everyone, rich and poor, educated and uneducated, young and old, celebrity and common people could contribute to the mission of cleanliness as per their abilities. Among the famous personalities selected for the said interactions included Amitabh Bachhan and Ratan Tata from Mumbai, Sat Guru from Coimbatore, Mata Amritamoyee from Chennai and so on. For representation of the common people of India from different fields in the interactions, he decided to have conversation with a girl student from the North East (Assam), few Jawans from Ladakh and two clergies from the Ajmer Sheriff among others.

Accordingly all the senior officers from my office were allotted the duty of facilitating the interactions with different group of persons at different places across the country. Being the dumbest among all the officers in the eyes of the boss, I was entrusted to take care of the direct telecasting from Ajmer Sheriff and Ouphulia Gaon of Dibrugarh District of Assam on that historical day of SBM unlike some of my colleagues who were allotted the work of facilitating the conversations with the likes of super star Amitabh Bachhan and Industrialist Ratan Tata from Gate Way of India, Mumbai.

In consultation with the Assam Government it was decided from Ouphulia Gaon of Dibrugarh, a girl student of Class XII would be interacting with the Honourable PM on that day. Similarly, from Ajmer Sheriff, two top clergies from two warring (or in mild words, competing groups) groups would be interacting with the Honourable PM Sir. So far these two places were concerned, the two places, more than two thousand five hundred km apart, have their own pros and cons and different types of challenges; one is at a rural place of a state which is known for lack of modern infra so far telecommunication is concerned; and the other one has problem of showing non-enthusiasm for the interaction with the Honourable PM Sir due to their own infighting between the groups of clergies of the Dargah and due to apparent ideological differences with the NDA Government. My boss was damn sure, I would fail to deliver and there would be another chance to humiliate me in front of my juniors.

The boss was right in his assessment of gravity of the problem at least in telecasting and interactions from the Dargah. At Ajmer Sheriff Dargah, inside the Dargah taking photograph was strictly prohibited and according to them there was no instance of any photography or videography that was ever done inside the premises of the Dargah (I cannot authenticate their claim from any other independent sources). Live interaction from the Dargah premises was immediately rejected by the Dargah Authority whose executive officer was a retired Government officer. To convince the authority, I was sent to meet the Dargah Authority and Ajmer Civil Administration. With lot of difficulty I was able to meet the CEO of the Dargah and the district administration of Ajmer. During my short visit in the first week of September, 2018 to the historical city of Ajmer, I met District Administration of Ajmer and Dargah authority with the request to join the nation-wise interactions of the Honourable Prime Minister. The DM was practically no clue how to convince the Dargah Authority to take part in the interactive session. But expectedly, the boss had more confidence in the powerful DM than in me.

However, powerless people have also some advantages over the powerful persons. Therefore, what the powerful boss and the all powerful DM could not do (might be because of their big ego), being powerless, I could do with my down to earth approach to convince the Dargah Authority to climb down from outright rejection to consider the offer in the right spirit. Finally, what the two powerful persons could not do, to convince the Dargah Authority to take part in the interactions, I was able to convince the Dargah Authority with folded hands to allow two clergies to take part from the Dargah premises in the live interaction with the Honourable PM on the designated day.

As it was negotiated by me, there was lot of doubt in the minds of the boss and his favourite group of officers on the successful interaction session with the Prime Minister, till the designated time on the designated day. However, on the D-day, to everyone's pleasant surprise, two clergies from the Dargah took part in the live telecast from within the premises of the Dargah and they had taken part in the discussion with the PM more than the allotted time of 90 seconds. Their actions only showed the overwhelming popularity of the Honourable PM and the eagerness of each and everyone to contribute to the mission of cleanliness of the country. In my personal opinion, much before, the visit of mine to the Dargah, the mission had penetrated into the minds of all the people of India irrespective of caste, creed, religion and region. As expected and may also be rightly so, no credit was given to me for my successful negotiation with the Dargah Authority and credit went to the DM and my boss for their enormous effort to make the programme a grand success.

As instructed by my boss, I went to Dibrugarh and remained present at Ouphulia Gaon from 12.09.2018 till the end of the programme to make the interactions with the school girl a grand success. During my stay at the village, I was privileged to witness something very special which I could not see in my entire service life.

From the 12th September, 2018 night I saw a festive mood gripping all the people living in the whole area of around 100 square KM. I was surprised to see the enthusiasm of the people where only one girl student was to interact with the Hon'ble PM. No doubt, she was the cynosure of all the people; it appeared she was the mythological princess for the people during those days and she was going to meet the mythological emperor of the country. Everyday people from various livelihood including the local MLA, Shri Bimal Bora (now he is a Cabinet Minister of Assam), District Administration headed by its young Deputy Commissioner, Ms. Loyela and both rich and poor common people of the area were toiling day and night to make the event a grand success. To my utter surprise, prior to the interaction session, the then CM of Assam, Shri Sarbananda Sonowal was also in constant touch with the local administration for making the interactive session a grand success.

On the D-day, at least 50,000 people thronged the entire area where only 5-10 thousand people were able to be accommodated inside the school field from where the girl student had to interact with the Hon'ble PM Sir. All the roads leading to the field, all the private courtyards of the neighbourhood were jam-packed with people from the early morning whereas the interaction time was fixed at around 8-30 AM only. The people of the neighbourhood were providing tea and snacks free of cost to the audience time to time. I was surprised to see the patience of the people in waiting for hours to have a glimpse of the PM on the screen, not in person.

Finally, the Hon'ble Prime Minister interacted with the girl student for about 105 seconds against the allotted time of 90 seconds asking different questions on cleanliness and use of toilets, people's participation in SBM etc. in the entire area of around 100 odd square KMs. Before and after the interaction, the Hon'ble PM Sir wished the people thronged in the field for their active participation in the Clean India Mission which was responded by thunderous applause from the audience of strong 50,000 local people. In fact, the people attended in the interactive session cheered the Hon'ble PM every time whenever his face was shown on the large screens placed on the field and on the roads for comfortable public viewing. I was surprised to see the sea of people who pledged to take part in clean India movement which the Hon'ble PM had led from the front.

Before finishing the episode of my visit to the village for the event, some of the facts about the backward village of Dibrugarh District, Ouphulia are shared below.

The village is a typical Assamese tribal village with majority of the people were Sonowal Kachari, a local tribe of Assam. In that village, even a couple of years ago, most of the tribal people were engaged in the business of selling local (illicit) country liquor to the passer by of other villages and drunkards from the nearby areas. But after declaration of Swachh Bharat Mission by the Hon'ble PM, they left their century long business of selling of local country liquor and started making and selling bamboo and cane products with innovative designs. This transformation was possible for their faith in PM's actions and at the initiation of some local NGOs who themselves were influenced by the inspirational actions of the Honourable PM. I had not visited that village prior to that particular visit, but what I saw in the village was that all the households were extremely clean and the village had achieved the target of 'hundred percent toilet coverage'. The village had a community sanitary complex at the market place which was donated by a young local businessman in memory of his father whom he lost at an early age. To my surprise, I could not see a single of piece of plastic in the entire area wherever I had ventured during three-four days of my stay whenever I visited one street to another one. In other words, an appeal of the Prime Minister and few sessions by some young boys and girls from the neighbouring villages made all the difference for the village. I felt to be a 'blessed one' for getting the opportunity to visit this village who was inspired by a visionary leader and in turn, the village had inspired thousands of villages of Assam to make themselves clean in the true sense.

During 2016 to 2019, we saw flurry of cultural programmes for publicity of SBM at the initiative of the Ministry. The cultural shows were organized through different event management groups depending upon the states who were hosting these events and magnitude of the programme. Some of the cultural shows during this period were mega events at national and international level mobilizing huge manpower and other resources. Many of these mega events were attended by none other than the Hon'ble PM himself showing his close involvement in the SBM scheme and his unflinching support for implementation of the scheme at the ground level. Without saying he was the main speaker of those events and he was also the main attraction for all those who had attended those events from different parts of the country and some times, different parts of the world. In these mega events each and every officer and each and every consultant had to be busy round the clock for six-seven days for each event. Even I alongwith other officers had to spend sometimes more than 20 hours at a stretch in the office though entire credit was apparently gone to the boss, as he was master in taking credit at the cost of others, sometimes even without uttering single 'thank you'. Every time before all the major National or International events, he used to dole one specific carrot before the officers and consultants, 'this time we shall have a group photograph with the PM Sir'. But every time he ensured that none of the officers and consultants including his apparent favourite 'Airforce', could not come 20 metres near to the

Honourable PM. However, I used to predict at the start of each of the Mega Event in front of the young officers and consultants that the boss would give a different excuse for not 'giving the carrot to eat by the proverbial donkeys in them'. Many used to agree with me and many were hoping against the hope to have a 'life time picture with the Honourable Prime Minister of India.'

To be fair to my boss, his leadership quality helped the Ministry to hold these mega events seamlessly and these mega events actually helped the Ministry to reach the common people of India and by the inspirational address by the PM had made immense impact in the minds of the audience who were forced to vow to make India clean. In these mega events not only the local people had joined, but also many people from all the states and UTs used to attend. Therefore, with each event, message of the Honourable PM Sir used to reach every nook and corner of the country. In fact PM was the ultimate ambassador of cleanliness, not only for India but also for the entire world, in general and for the third world countries, in particular. Each and every leader of the third world countries, looked for the advice of our beloved PM Sir to make their country also ODF. From UN to other World Organizations were thankful to him for the stupendous achievement by India in reducing the OD status of the world as a whole. In one of the events

Secretary General of UN praised Honourable Prime Minister of India for his extra-ordinary leadership on India's achievement in reducing OD status of the entire world. In another mega event at New Delhi, PM Sir was joined by the President of World Bank in hailing the participation of the common people in the implementation of Swachh Bharat Mission.

Other than these central level mega events, a lot of state level, district level, block level, Panchayat level and village level events were organised to motivate people to construct toilets, to use regularly these toilets and to keep the surroundings of the households, villages clean. Through these cultural events, the benefits of use of toilets were showcased for the benefits of the rural people of India.

To involve and to encourage the grassroots level officials in the mission, the Hon'ble PM had decided to write personal letters to Panchayat Secretaries and Sarpanches. To arrange the logistic to send around 2.5 lakh letters in one week time, a firm was engaged. Sending around 2.5 lakh letters was nothing sort of a herculean task for the Ministry. Thanks to the sincere involvement of all the officers and all the consultants of the Ministry, this massive work had been completed in time to the satisfaction of the all concerned. One can imagine the joy of getting a personal letter by name from the PM of

India. This act of PM Sir had created immense influence in the psyche of the Panchayat Secretaries/ Sarpanches, irrespective of party affiliation of those officials/ elected members of the Gram Panchayats of all over the country.

However, when it was decided to send personal letters by the PM Sir to some celebrities in each of the states, a Faux Pa was came to forefront for me. All the state Governments were requested to send a list of thirty celebrities for the purpose of sending signed letters of the Hon'ble PM Sir. As per the request, like other state governments, the line department of Government Assam also sent a list of 30 celebrities. As I was travelling to Ajmer on that particular day, true to my callous approach for anything and everything in the official works spanning over thirty odd years, without verifying the names forwarded by the State Government, I forwarded to the consultant who was compiling the list of celebrities. The consultant instead of asking me about the veracity of the list, he informed my boss that one name amongst the 30 names from Assam was of mine. My boss got another chance to mock me for the next two years for that Faux Pa. Whom do you blame for the Faux Pa? I squarely blame myself only for my casual approach in dealing with such a sensitive issue.

It has already been shared with all of you that unfortunately except for few elite Indians, most of the people of India who took birth before the advent of 21st century have the ignominy of defecating in open at least once in their life time. As already said, even though my father's residence was only 100 metres away from the National Highway and one KM away from the central point of the town, tap connection for drinking water had been installed only in December, 2020 after JJM was implemented in Assam from 2019 alongwith other parts of the country. Though, I have seen from my childhood days that my ancestral house was located only 100 metres away from the last water supply stand-post, it remained in the same position for the last fifty odd years without any improvement on the ground. Beyond my ancestral residence, all the residences of my village and all the villages away from the central point of my home town did not have any tap connection for drinking water till December, 2020 despite the fact that Assam is not a water-starved state unlike Rajasthan or Bundel Khand Region of UP/MP. However, like many villages of Assam, my area is also an iron effected area and therefore, it is wrong to say that we did not feel the necessity of a functional tap water connection in our household. 'Better late than never' is the apt statement for the Assamese people so far functional tap water is concerned. Now in Assam also more than 35% rural households have been provided with functional tap water since the beginning of JJM in the state.

I took lot of time after joining in the Department of Drinking Water and Sanitation to understand properly the problem of open defecation in some of the states of India. I was aware that in Assam and in other North Eastern States of India, some people used to go for open defecation due to poor economic status, but not due to any mental block to go to a toilet for defecation. Therefore, most of the residents of these states welcome the move of the Central Government and the State Governments to provide toilets whole heartedly without any reservations against construction of toilets except few isolated pockets. Wherever there were some exceptions even in the North East Region, a few of those will be described at appropriate place. On the other hand, many people of some of the other states thought otherwise and in the first two years after launching the scheme nationwide. In some of the places in those states, the resistance for construction was mild; but in some places, these anti- toilet construction lobbies put forward a strong resistance; particularly for construction of toilets within their premises. For the first time, I heard a sentence with lot of intrinsic meaning, 'Audi to OD.' The background story of this sentence goes like this:

There was a Zamindaar (landlord) in a village of Western UP with lots of movable and immovable properties. He had seven cars including two Audi cars. These two Audi cars were used to transport their family members to a secluded place in the early morning and after dusk for defecating in open. The palatial building with more than twenty living rooms did not have any toilet. However, for the guests coming from outside the villages, attached beautiful toilets with all modern facilities were available in their guest house which was located in the same compound, but detached from the main palatial building. If any member (particularly female member) had to go to the toilet at day time, they used to go to the toilets of the guest house reluctantly as they felt suffocated inside four walls of a toilet and they also used to think going to open for defecating was healthier practice than defecating in a closed room.

After few sessions of counselling by the Swachhagrahis and other state Government officials, they reluctantly constructed twenty attached toilets in their palatial building spending almost a crore of rupees. Ladies of the family first stopped going outside for defecation. The oldest member of the family was the last man to use the attached toilet and the story of 'Audi to OD' ends there with a proverbial 'happy ending of a Hindi film story.'

Might be the above story was a fictitious one, but what I am going to tell you a real story where I was also an actor to perform my limited role as an 'extra' in a commercial Hindi Masala movie just after few months of joining into the Ministry of Drinking Water and Sanitation in 2016.

As I was new to the Ministry, I visited a village in Bihar along with the concerned BDO of a block where the village was situated, against the existing protocol of the Ministry; not to go beyond District HQs by a senior officer. Actually I committed that 'grave' mistake as I worked earlier in NSSO (National Statistics Survey Organization) where officers had to visit some households of the selected village/ UFS (Urban Frame Survey) block (UFS block is different from administrative block which is maximum of 1 square KM in size and with population of 600-1200) while inspecting the work of a subordinate in a village/ UFS block. For breaking the protocol, expectedly, I was admonished by my boss in front of all the officers as if I had committed a 'grave crime' not a mistake, per se. However, visiting to the village to see the construction of toilets became a norm of the day for the Ministry of Drinking Water and Sanitation after a series of meeting with the Honourable MPs in September-October, 2016 in the Parliament House Annexe at the behest of the Hon'ble PM sir. I have mentioned this part of my experience in the Ministry to highlight, why earlier schemes relating to toilet construction and other schemes aim to uplift the poor people of India had failed miserably and schemes including SBM succeeded under Modi Government. Probably for the first time since Independence, in Modi regime, the top officers started to visit backward villages of India to see the implementation of the welfare schemes of the Government. Now we can see the difference in implementation of the schemes in the present regime with earlier regimes due to a simple change of the mind-sets of the senior officers (or forced change of mind-sets) to visit the backward villages by the very senior officers themselves instead of relying on the reports of the juniors, many of whom might be totally corrupt.

Coming to my visit to a village of District Patna with the BDO, the village official who accompanied us told that one of the richest men of the village refused to construct a toilet in his newly constructed house. The village official led to a large two storied RCC building under construction, which was almost complete when I had visited the village in August 2016. The owner of the building was not present when the team of officers reached the building, probably to avoid a confrontation with the Government officials led by a BDO (I might be a non-entity for him), he slipped out from the village. However, the wife appeared before the officers when someone had called her from her neighbour's house. She was a lady of early forties with beautiful attire on her beautiful body as observed by me with my hawk eyes. When BDO wanted to know whether the information about not keeping any provision of any toilet in the building was true or not, she confirmed about the authenticity of the information given by the village official.

'Why?' The BDO asked the lady.

'Why should we keep provision for toilets when we have our own open fields of few acres of land? We have our own priorities to spend our hard earned money.' She countered the officer.

With lot of patience the officer explained the middle aged lady why construction and use of toilets are good for health and environment.

She gave her counter argument, 'we have to send our son to college and we need lot of money for that. We have lot of land properties and we never go to other's field to defecate. What is the problem of the Government if we do not construct toilets?'

Slowly their arguments became hot and hotter and finally the BDO thundered, 'I am from – caste and you are also from the same -- caste. If you do not construct your toilet within next one month, I shall make sure that you are not going to get any benefit of any of Government schemes so long I am here as the BDO.'

That warning of the BDO silenced the lady at that point of time and we left the place. However, I could not be able to know how long time actually they took to construct a toilet. But for the first time, I understood, the SBM could not be a mission of constructing toilets, it was beyond that. From that day onwards, I understood that SBM was not only a mission of construction of toilets, but also was a mission to change the mindset for the crores of people of India for making India clean and as the first step towards achieving total cleanliness, the mission was to make India an ODF country.

I was informed by an officer of a particular state that, a Central Government Minister hailing from the same state once pissed on the floor of the Domestic Terminal of Indira Gandhi International Airport in the year of 2012 even after lot of persuasion by the lady escort officer from Indian Airlines. I cannot authenticate whether that was a true story or just a concocted story by someone who used to dislike that particular Minister because of his social background.

I grew up in my village and college hostel hearing such type of stories about our Hon'ble Ministers visiting abroad. I did not believe those stories at all a few years back till I myself experienced some awkward moments during my official visits to the residences of some extremely rich people of some of the places of some states at the beginning of launching of Swachh Bharat Mission in 2015. After those visits, I started believing those stories (or simple jokes) at least partially; if not fully.

I need not have to emphasize, that the young ones, particularly students had played a pivotal role in changing the mindset of the elderly people who had lot of hesitation in construction and use of the constructed toilets in some places of India. Even the people of the generation who were born in between 1960 to 2005, but still not very much enthusiastic about maintaining cleanliness around their surrounding have a lot to learn from the young ones. Therefore, I shall share some of the stories which are evolved around my field visits and these angels who were actively associated with the actions to make India ODF and clean.

Let me go once again to Ouphulia Gaon of Dibrugarh District, Assam to share an experience of mine during my stay in the village. In one evening during my off and on visit to the village from Dibrugarh City where I was accommodated from 12th September to 16th September, while I was taking tea in a roadside small tea stall, I saw two young boys of around eight- nine years were coming towards the tea stall where I was taking a cup of tea. When they were about 50 metres away from me, they took out two chocolates from their pockets and peeled the wrappers and started eating the chocolates. Remembering my own good childhood days, I was expecting the young boys would throw the wrappers casually to the roadside as I and my friends used to do without any remorse or any guilt feeling in our childhood days. But what I saw in the next one minute was an eye opener for me. Both the boys crossed the road and put the wrappers in the dustbin made of bamboo. Bamboo dustbins were placed in every 100 metres throughout the village. I simply compared my own behaviour towards cleanliness in my childhood days with the behaviour towards cleanliness of these young ones. My head automatically bowed to the unknown boys of remote Ouphulia Gaon of Assam with respect and awe.

The next episode I had experienced in a village of Nagpur district; which was not as remote as Ouphulia Gaon of Assam. I was to attend a meeting at Nagpur alongwith some of my senior officers of my Department including my boss. The boss was about to reach Nagpur from another city of Maharashtra by 12 Noon and on the other hand I reached Nagpur by morning flight from Delhi at around 8-30 AM. As I was fond of visiting villages of India at any time, with the permission of my boss, I visited few villages of Nagpur district between 9 AM to 12 Noon on that day.

Like any other God fearing man, though not a very religious one, when my escort officer requested me to visit a temple, I could not say a 'no' to the request of the escorting officer and went to the temple premises. The temple was full of visitors and there I met few children also who were not visitors of the temple but were selling flowers and other materials normally used by the devotees while submitting their obeisance to the deity of the temple. I asked one of them casually, 'why have you not gone to school today?'

With a lovely smile the young girl replied, 'uncle you are becoming old, today is Sunday.'

With a grin, I replied back, 'You are right. I am your grandpa's age.'

She was a talkative girl, 'No, he is little older than you.' I felt good on her reply that she thought I was younger than her grandfather.

'May I ask you a question, if you do not mind?'

She nodded.

'Do you have a toilet at your home (I deliberately avoided to use the technical word, premises)?'

'Yes, we have two toilets in our home. One was constructed by my father for our family a few years ago and the second was given to my grandfather by the Government.' She replied with a pride in her voice.

'So, none of your family members goes out for defecating and all of you are using your toilets. Am I right?' The NSSO genie came alive in me.

'No uncle; our grandpa is not using the toilet regularly. He uses the toilet only during rainy season.' With visibly an uncomfortable smile she replied.

'Why do you not stop him from going to open defecation?' I asked her with a comforting voice.

'We are trying for the last one year to stop him from going to the open field (for defecation). He and his old friends argue with us that they feel suffocated inside the toilets. It is an old habit for them, and therefore it may take little longer to cultivate the habit of using toilets. Uncle, do you have a toilet?' She asked me a pertinent question.

When I told her that I had one, she asked me again with another innocent smile on her face, 'Do you use it regularly?'

When I said a 'yes' to her question she advised me, 'Uncle always use your toilet. It is a healthy practice; everyone should follow.'

'How do you know (that it is a healthy practice) ?' I wanted to know from the young girl.

'My teacher says. Moreover, we see in the TV, all the great people are saying why we should use toilets and why we should not go for open defecation.' She explained to me. Probably, she also explained these things to her grandfather also; I thought.

On asking her who the great people she was referring, she uttered the names of few before me, 'Modiji, Amitabhji, Fandavezji and many others. I saw the film, Toilet: Ek Prem Katha with my family when it was shown in our Panchayat hall. It was so funny. Have you seen the movie?'

I wanted to boast, I saw the premier of the movie as an honoured guest, but instead, I said, 'yes I saw it in my computer.'

'So, you know how to use a computer. I also know, but my grandfather does not know anything about a computer.' She said with another beautiful smile.

When I left the temple premises after half an hour, I realized our country is in the safe hands of our next generations.

During one of my visits to Bihar, at Nalanda, I met a group of students at the Budh-stupa who were coming from some villages of Bihar on an excursion. I asked one of them, where from young boy had come. After knowing that they were from a village from West Champaran (Betiya), I asked him, 'I heard that your district is very near to the Nepal border. Is it true?'

'Yes uncle.' He replied with a smile.

‘How is your village? Do you like your village?’ I wanted to know something about his village.

‘Yes and no. Yes, because it is a complete green village unlike many villages of Bihar. ‘No’, because, it is not an ‘ODF village.’ The answer of the young boy had floored me. His answer silenced me for few seconds.

‘Do you know, what is an ODF village?’ After getting my wits back I asked the small boy, standing tall before me.

‘Yes uncle. When all the people of the village will have toilets and all the villagers will use the toilets, then village will be an ODF village. In our village hardly 70% households are having toilets and those having toilets are also not using always.’ His knowledge about ODF had really given me a pleasant surprise, though official definition of ODF was little different from what the young boy was saying.

‘How do you know so much about cleanliness?’

‘From our school teacher, uncle, he taught us about cleanliness, ODF etc. He even goes to the elderly villagers to tell about cleanliness etc. Many listens to him and many ignore his advices. But most of us listen to him and we try our best to convince our parents to follow the advices of our teacher.’ He concluded.

‘Is he here?’

‘Yes uncle, he is with us.’ Then young boy called and introduced his teacher to me.

After their small introduction, the teacher told me that he attended the conference of the Swachhagrahis held at Champaran which was addressed by the Hon’ble Prime Minister Modiji on 10.04.2017 coinciding with the centenary of Champaran Satyagraha against the exploitation of the Indigo planters.

I knew about the meeting which was attended by more than two lakh people including more than ten thousand Sachhagrahis from other states/ UTs associated with SBM in different capacities. Though for arranging the logistics I was sent to Champaran two months before the conclave, I had to stay back in the office on the day of the conclave on the advice of my smart boss on some pretext.

Prior to the conclave when I visited the state alongwith a lady consultant I had the opportunity to see the active participation of the common people to make their villages ODF.

During that visit, as a late riser, I was little bit annoyed when the consultant requested me to get up early in the morning, at around 4 AM to go to a village to see the early morning activities of the ‘Nighrani Samiti’ constituted in a village to see how the committee tried to make the villagers understand the ill effects of open defecation and their efforts to stop the practice of open defecation in their village. I was about to tell her to go alone in the morning and report me about her village visit; but my inner voice stopped me in doing so and on the next morning I alongwith the consultant and few officers from the state government visited the village. When we reached the village, at 4-30 in the early morning, to my pleasant surprise, at least hundred persons including some teen-aged children were present there to meet us. Looking at their enthusiasm I understood that 'none can stop this movement now till it achieves its goal of making India open defecation free.'

On that day only, I came to know how 'Nighrani Samiti' of the village took the pain to make the adamant 'OD goer' understand the ill effects of the OD and how they had to be vigil to stop the people from going for OD in the early morning for months together.

According to me, majority of the people from 'so called mainland India' have lot of misconceptions about the people of North East, barring Assam. According to me, even many people outside North East may not be aware that majority of Assamese are non-tribal and Assam comprised of two valleys, Brahmaputra valley and Barak valley and therefore Assam is a state having mostly plain areas barring undivided Karbi Anglong district dividing the two valleys.

In the hindsight, being from Assam, I must also admit that Assam is as dirty or as clean as any other main land states of India contrary to the other North Eastern States of India which are mainly hilly areas, are cleaner and greener than rest of the country including Assam and Tripura, upto some extent. Except Tripura, densities of population of the other North Eastern States are very less compared to Assam and other states of India. Arunachal Pradesh has the least per KM population with only 23 Lakh people in 81, 000 sq KM area according to 2011 population census. All the indigenous people of these hilly states of North East have developed the habit of going to toilet long before SBM was launched in other parts of the country though due to financial constraints, most of the toilets were not safe toilets as have been propagated by the International agencies and Government of India through SBM. Because of their mindset towards cleanliness, those who were aware about this fact they did not show any surprise when Sikkim became the first ODF state in the country, even though construction of any infrastructure is a challenge in these areas due to high material and labour cost. One can have an idea from the following example of price escalation of a single item, a bag of cement; as one goes up to the different places of Arunachal Pradesh the price of cement goes up exponentially.

Price of a bag of cement at Bandar Dewa (a border town of Assam) was Rs 400/- (in 2017 as I was told during my visit to the state) which went up to Rs.450 at Itanagar, capital town of Arunachal Pradesh. The same bag of cement had to be purchased at around Rs.2000/-by a customer at a village bordering China. The prices of other construction materials were also escalated as it went to upper parts of the state in the similar proportion.

Unlike in other states of India, if a person used to go for OD in these states, it was not because of his sweet will, but because of some compelling reasons which might range from poverty to non availability of toilets on a journey from one place to another place through a sparsely populated hilly terrain. However, even on the high ways in these states, existence of more neat and clean toilets could be seen compared to other places of India including that of Assam much before implementation of SBM. That was a clear indication of the mentality of these people so far cleanliness was concerned despite of having many obstacles in keeping the roadside toilets clean for the travellers.

After launching of Swachh Bharat Mission, some of the major challenges in these states to make all the villages ODF and maintain the ODF status were high cost of construction materials, logistics to reach the villages, non-availability of local skilled persons for construction and maintenance of these toilets. To meet these challenges, some of the North Eastern states immediately had raised the state share for incentive money from RS.12000/- to Rs.18000/- to the beneficiaries. To solve the problems of non-availability of bricks, cements and iron rods few young educated men came forward with some innovative ideas and some innovative techniques to construct safe toilets with locally available materials. For example, in Arunachal Pradesh, with the active technical help from these young qualified men, the local people started using boulders instead of bricks and bamboo products instead of iron rods for construction of safe and lasting toilets. Similarly, in Mizoram, Nagaland and Tripura, corrugated sheets were used extensively to reduce the burden of cement and iron rods which are relatively scarce and costly compared to corrugated sheets. In Nagaland, the authorities provided the raw materials of Rs. 12000/- at the construction sites leaving the owners of the toilets to construct toilets according to their choices. Through this act, Nagaland Government tried to infuse the sense of ownership in the psyche of the beneficiaries. Whatever might be the innovative ideas coming from the public, young educated people it was only because of making of cleanliness of the villages, including making the villages ODF, a

'Jan Andolan' in these states, might came little earlier than some other states of India. Not surprisingly, Sikkim became the first ODF state of the country and Arunachal was also not far behind even though it was an extremely sparsely populated state with difficult terrain. As expectedly, Tripura and Assam took maximum time to declare themselves ODF states due to prevailing socio-political reasons. Though, I did not observe any resistance from public and political dispensation in implementation SBM in Assam, I observed total non-cooperation of the Government in Tripura and from 74% coverage of toilets in 2011 census became standstill without single percentage improvement till a favourable Government was installed in Tripura in 2017. I was sent to Tripura more than 10 times in the next two years to help the SBM implementing officials of Tripura Government to make Tripura ODF by 2nd October, 2019. Only God knows whether my visit helped Tripura to declare themselves as an ODF state much before the target date or only because of the getting up from the slumbers by the state Government officials to 'declare themselves as ODF'. Nevertheless, I enjoyed my visits to all the districts of Tripura, meeting the ground level officers and the villagers of different communities during those visits.

I was the only privileged officer of Government of India to attend the function hosted by

Arunachal Government to declare themselves as an ODF state. It was a grand function which was attended by no less than 5 cabinet ministers of the state and which was presided over by the Chief Minister himself. The young dashing CM, Pema Khandu gave a very inspiring lecture where he told the audience about the challenges faced by the State for making the state ODF. However, the most interesting address was delivered by one of the Cabinet Ministers where he highlighted as a young village boy from a poor family how much problems and humiliations, he had to face for not having a toilet in his residence. He recounted the horrific stories how the pet dogs of his village were after the young boys and girls whenever they squatted for defecating in the open. He thanked Honourable PM for thinking for the dignity of the poor people of the country by announcing about the SBM from the walls of the Red Fort and his constant monitoring of the mission over the years despite being criticised by many self-styled intellectuals of India and abroad.

I had been the only privileged officer to meet all the Chief Ministers of North East during some functions or otherwise and have long discussions for making these states ODF before 2nd October, 2019. All the Chief Ministers of North Eastern states showed their appreciations for the yeoman services of the Zila Swachhata Preraks (or Tata Preraks) sponsored by the Tata Group.

According to all the CMs of NE, these youngsters were extremely intelligent and dedicated even though many of them were not local youths. Many of them were first timer to these states and were coming from a complete different social and financial environment. Because of their whole hearted involvement in the mission, many local NGOs were also inspired and they also did their best in achieving the common goal of achieving ODF status by 2nd October, 2019 as envisaged by the Hon'ble PM of India. However, most of the CMs showed their unhappiness to know that unilateral decision of the Ministry of Drinking Water and Sanitation (or was it a decision of a particular officer who wanted to take the entire credit to make India ODF?) to terminate their services after the states declared themselves as ODF states. At that time, the persons at the helm of affairs of the department could not see the challenges of sustaining ODF status in the villages where poverty and natural disasters including flood have more control over the hapless poor people in the countryside than their will to keep their surroundings clean. However, luckily after exit of some officers from the Department, a new set of officers took over and the present dispensation in the department realised the necessity of keeping a strict vigil on these villages to avoid slip back of the ODF villages to OD villages in due course of time.

However, I strongly believe that some young professionals in the line of Tata Preraks should be engaged for sustaining ODF status in these states. But will anyone hear the idea of keeping young professionals for sustaining ODF status in the rural parts of the country?

To my satisfaction and few likeminded officers from these states, kept some of these young professionals to sustain the ODF status in their states as their contractual employees. Perhaps you may be interested to know, if I have any role in keeping these youngsters in these states; the answer is a resounding 'no'. In this case, credit goes to the State Authorities of the concerned states and Federal Structure of the Country.

Role and contributions of International Organizations, Indian NGOs, Corporate Houses and Individuals who have lot of influence amongst the masses had been massive in achieving the goal of making India ODF by 2nd October, 2019. Among the International Organizations, UNICEF, World Bank, Melinda and Gates Foundations have lot of contribution in making India an ODF country much before the target date of SDG (Sustainable Development Goals) in 2030. In Indian context, Tata Group of Industries led by philanthropist Ratan Tata and personalities like Mata Amritmoyee, Amitabh Bachhan, Sachin Tendulkar, Actor Akshay Kumar etc. had lot of contribution to motivate people to make India clean. A good number of PSUs had also contributed for this national cause by taking over different projects in the iconic places spreading over the entire country, like Kamakhya Mandir of Guwahati, Golden Temple of Punjab, Somnath Temple of Gujarat, Minakshi Temple of Tamil Nadu, Ajmer Sheriff of Rajasthan, Taj Mahal of Uttar Pradesh etc.

However, the contribution of Tata Trust had been much more compared to all other NGOs in my eyes as Tata Trust not only help the Ministry of Drinking Water and Sanitation by donating money but also providing few hundreds of young professionals to the Ministry for more than two years.

About 450 young professionals (known as Zila Swachhata Preraks or shortly Tata Preraks) were appointed by the Tata Group of companies because of an understanding between Government of India and Tata Group of Industries and due to coming together for a noble cause of two great visionaries of modern India, Hon'ble PM of India and the former Chairman of the Tata Sons, Ratan Naval Tata who is not only a mere Indian industrialist, but also a renown philanthropist of the entire world. Shri Ratan Tata, even at the age of 80 is still the head of charitable trusts of Tata Sons.

Originally, Tata Groups wanted to provide at least one Zila Prerak in each district of the country as agreed by Tata group of Industries. However, might be due to reluctance of some state governments and some reservations on the part of my boss, even at the highest point of time, number of Zilla Prerak could not cross the magic figure of 500 against 700 plus districts of India. However, India should be thankful to these 450 odd Tata Preraks for their invaluable services to the nation for making India almost an ODF country much before the expectations of the whole world.

These young professionals were attached to the DMs/ DCs of the allotted districts to assist not only in the technical matters but also in making policy matters so far providing toilets and changing the mindsets of the reluctant people, if any to achieve ODF status for the districts. As these young professionals were from different disciplines, their contributions to the allotted districts were immense in their fields. For example, if the young professional was an engineer, alongwith other works his/ her background became very handy in innovation on construction of toilets with locally available materials. If the young professional was from commerce background he/ she became an asset for the administration in judicious allocation of funds in different blocks, preparation of budgets etc. If the young professional was from social science background, he/ she became one of the chief motivators of the district for use of toilets by the reluctant people for the allotted district.

This group of young professionals served their allotted districts from two to three years depending upon when the district declared itself ODF. Sometimes some of the professionals were shifted from one district to another district depending upon the specific necessity of a particular district and educational background of the young professional. Power of transfer of these young professionals within the state was vested with the State Government and interstate transfer was done by the administration of Tata Sons in consultation with the then Ministry of Drinking Water and Sanitation.

Though, the contribution of these young professional was immense in terms of construction of toilets, in motivating people to construct toilets and most importantly, in some states, motivating the people to use the newly constructed toilets with Government finance, they were slowly but steadily given 'pink slip' by their employer, perhaps (as doubted by many including me), on the advice of a self-centred but very powerful officer, to full-fill his some hidden agenda and safeguard his own interest. As the powerful officer left the Government, he made sure none of these youngsters should remain in the service who could have been immense help, in my opinion, for their services for maintaining and sustaining ODF status of the villages and for implementation of ODF plus scheme launched by the department subsequently. Unfortunately, as stated above almost all the young professionals barring a few handpicked young professionals were given 'pink slip' immediately after 2nd October, 2019. As a result of that the 'misses' could not be properly addressed by the Ministry and the state governments which culminated adverse results on coverage of toilets in some major surveys conducted by some reputed Government Agencies like NSSO and NFHS-5. However, some of the state governments perhaps have the same arguments that of mine and they had accommodated some of the young professionals and fortunately these young professionals are still contributing a lot in achieving the vision of the Hon'ble PM of total cleanliness for our country.

NB: If anyone who matters in the Government and Tata Sons by chance reads this book, may please consider the observations made by me to get the services of such young professionals for sometimes in near future for achieving and maintaining true ODF and make India cleaner and healthier.

After these serious observations made by me, let us peep into some of the experiences gained by me with these professionals placed under different state governments.

Let us start with my first encounter with the Preraks in the VIP guest house, Agartala, Tripura. From their body language I could understand they cannot be from Government of Tripura as I knew many Government officers from Tripura when I was posted in a different Department of a different Ministry. There were all together four young persons, out of which three were young, brave and energetic ladies with different personalities. The young man appeared to be smart and a local young man of around 25. My assumption was found to be correct; he was a local boy, having very good knowledge of local politics, local work culture and other local geo-political environment prevailing in the state. Out of the three young ladies, one was from the home state, Tripura, one was originally from Uttarakhand but based in West Bengal and therefore fluent in Bengali and Hindi. But I found the third one most interesting, very soft spoken and miserly in opening up her thoughts. Anyhow, all of them informed me about reluctance in the bureaucracy in implementing the SBM in the scheme alongwith lack of political will actually hampered the progress of the scheme.

However, in the second visit, these young professionals told me that following the

Newton's first law of motion, with great efforts from the young professionals, the State Government officials also got up from their slumbers and the political will for implementation of SBM had also taken place. They were hundred percent correct in their assessment as the speed of construction of toilets picked up within few months of their association with the State Government officials. After breaking their initial inertia of these officers they were able to motivate the people to take part in the Jan Andolan which had already swept other parts of the country. Within one and half years, all the districts of Tripura were able to declare themselves ODF where the toilet coverage was standstill at 74% for more than six years from 2011 to 2017.

I was aware that the Tata Preraks were doing very well in Arunachal much before I met them in December, 2016 at Itanagar. They were praised not only by the officers but also praised by all the politicians whom I met during three to four visits I had made to the beautiful state bordering China during that period. The dashing young Hon'ble Chief Minister, Shri Pema Khandu conveyed his appreciations and thanks for these young professionals to the PM sir and Shri Ratan Tata through my boss. However, I was very doubtful whether the message of appreciations of the Hon'ble CM of Arunachal were conveyed to the PM sir and Ratan Tata or not; as I wrongly or rightly, doubted the intent of my boss, My boss always wanted to impress upon everyone that he and his wife were the only responsible persons in the entire country to make India ODF. No doubt, my boss had been always good in managing the media in projecting himself as the main pillar of the project, SBM even sometimes undermining the contribution and vision of the Hon'ble PM Sir. It might be an assessment of mine which perhaps none including my other colleagues will believe.

Coming to the Preraks of Arunachal Pradesh, some of them were shifted to Assam and Nagaland once all the districts of Arunachal declared themselves ODF. This group of Tata Preraks helped Assam and Nagaland also in their march towards declaring themselves ODF before second October, 2019.

A few of the Preraks were posted at the Departmental HQs also to help the SBM sections and my boss directly. They were given more importance than even the senior officers of the Department to the utter disgust of some of the senior officers including that of me. They were nick-named in the department as 'Air Force of the big boss.' However, true to his colour, my boss made sure that they got their 'pink slips' one or two days before his exit from the Department and Government of India. On this, I recalled a story of 'two bullocks and a pig' that I read in my childhood days on the ‘pink slip’ episode of these pampered Preraks (except one Prerak, whom he accommodated in some other organisation) and shunting out of some ‘Air Force’ consultants before the unceremonious exit of my boss. The story goes like this:

A farmer had two bullocks that were used to till his fields for his cultivation. One day, the wife of the farmer brought a pig to their home. From that day onwards, all the members of the farmer started taking more care of the pig than their hard working and faithful bullocks. Upset with the behaviour of the farmer family, one evening the young bullock ventilated his anguish before the older one, ‘how ungrateful our owner’s family is! We toiled our days and night in the fields during the cultivating season to increase their family income; but look at their behaviour towards the pig now which was brought just two weeks before the harvest festival!’

The old bullock smiled and remarked, ‘Wait till the morning of the festival day and you will know whether the family members of our owner grateful to us or not.’

On the festive day, in the early morning the bullocks were bathed, garlanded, given the choicest of their food to eat and worshipped as the main deity of the family and took their blessings for a prosperous life for the entire family. The family also asked for the forgiveness of the bullocks if the family had hurt their sentiments by their actions in the whole year prior to the harvesting festive day. The older bullock asked the younger one, 'Are you happy now?'

'Yes, brother; but still I could not understand in the last three weeks why we were given less importance than the pig by the family.' The younger bull was still confused at the behaviour of the farmer's family.

'Wait till the evening. All your confusing questions will be answered.'

As expected by the older bullock, the pig was killed and the farmer's family alongwith their guests enjoyed the meat covered with lot of fats (because of good feeding of the pig for the last three weeks lot of fats around its muscles accumulated). The younger bull got his answer why the pig was fed so well in the last three weeks.

I remained in the Department even after the unceremonious exit of my boss and I was still contributing something as per my capability till the date of my retirement. On the other hand pampered 'Air Force of my boss' had to leave the Department without a fuss and practically, they were left high and dry to their fate like well-designed costly paper plates thrown into a dustbin after taking only one lunch or dinner.

However, I sometimes become upset when someone informs me that some of the Preraks (including some of the pampered ones) are now unemployed or underemployed.

During my visit to Kerala I had to face a question when I was delivering a lecture on the ill effects of open defecation. From the perplexed faces of the young boys and girls present in the meeting, I could very easily understand that they were almost at a loss to understand the meaning of 'OD' and 'ODF' I was trying to explain with my rustic English. After explaining once again what OD was, one of the young boys asked me, 'how it is possible to defecate in the open, sir? It must be a very disgraceful act and it is against the dignity of a man or woman. I think it is a hypothetical situation you are trying to explain to us in the present context.'

Before I could answer on his question and on his trash comment, another boy from behind told him, 'a few -- people who were working as labourers in some local factories used to defecate in the open even after they were provided with toilets by their factory owners. After getting complaints from the local people, they were arrested by the police once and many of them have stopped now, but still some of them are going to the fields for defecating.'

I understood that the local people of Kerala had stopped long back the bad habit of going to the open for defecating; but due to some migrant labourers, the problem of OD was prevalent in the vicinity of the factories.

The statement of the boy reminded me of the statement of one of the Additional Secretary who was from Assam cadre but hailed from UP told once, 'Assam could have been long back ODF, but because of the migrants from -- and - have created herculean task for Assam Government to make Assam an ODF state.'

Similar sentiment was echoed by the officials of Gujarat Government when I had to visit Gujarat during the same period.

Though, the Ministry of Drinking Water and Sanitation had never advocated use of force to stop people from defecating in the open, some of the local authorities had to enforce it due to public pressure from some of the effected localities.

Coming back to my visit to Kerala, I had learnt many things from the people of Kerala how people can keep their surroundings neat and clean. During my several visits to different villages of the State, I realized due to level of education, migration to other developed countries, the people of Kerala understood the necessity of keeping the villages clean and for that use of toilets was a must condition (necessary condition in mathematical language) for all the villagers.

However, in the neighbouring Karnataka and Tamilnadu, in those days, the situation on ground in respect of toilet coverage and use of toilet were not that bright. Thanks to the Jan Andolon, the brain child of the Hon'ble PM, these two states were also able to declare themselves ODF states much before 2nd October, 2019.

Though I promised earlier that I shall not mention any name of the concerned officers, I cannot stop praising the efforts and sincerity of Shri Laxmipati, MD, Tamil Nadu and Mrs. Bimla of Karnataka in their journey towards declaration of ODF of their respective states by themselves. Similarly, Dr. Siddharth Singh, MD Assam, Shri Pratul Choudhury, State Coordinator of Assam, Shri Partha Barua, State Coordinator of Assam and Shri S. Barua, Chief Engineer of Assam had lot of contribution for making Assam ODF. Except one or two DCs of Assam, all the DCs helped the PHE Department to make Assam ODF.

Few best officers from our Department were entrusted the duties of making UP and Bihar ODF before 2nd October, 2019 by my boss. These officers made countless travels to these two states to mobilize and motivate people to construct toilets and use of the toilets once the toilets were constructed. With their efforts alongwith the efforts of the officers of State Government, tireless efforts of the Scwachhagrahis and Sarpanches, a wave of Jan Andolan was generated in these two states. Finally, these two states were able to declare themselves 'officially ODF' before 2nd October, 2019. Unfortunately, through some advertisements UP Government had later on contradicted their own declaration of being UP as a whole an ODF state. Nevertheless the total number of construction toilets in UP was a massive success without iota of doubt. I sincerely hope this state becomes a real ODF state as of now after three years of formally declared themselves as ODF state. Incidentally, UP is one of the largest states which I was not allowed to visit in my entire period of posting in the Department for pushing progress in the direction of attaining ODF status or for inspection of National Annual Rural Survey on Sanitation (NARSS). NARSS was conducted consecutively for three years at the behest of World Bank. Though World Bank had paid only a peanut of the total expenditure spent on toilet construction activities, they tried to overwhelm the Department with thousands of questions and restrictions like they used to do when India was struggling for every single penny few years ago. Thanks to earlier affiliations of my boss and his intent to go back to the World Bank, the

Department had to heed all the unsolicited tantrums of the officials of World Bank as usual. I also had to accompany one of the top officials of the World Bank to a village of UP in the year 2018 as directed by my boss.

However, later on, after exit of my earlier boss from the Government, I got an opportunity to make a visit to Varanasi as a part of delegation of NITI Ayog in September, 2020 for a meeting. Though I was there only for 24 hours, I found the Varanasi block was extremely advance in terms of all the parameters of cleanliness. Again unfortunately, when I made a visit to Prayagraj and Varanasi Districts to see the progress of JJM, I found there was a wide gap between actual toilet coverage in these two districts (except perhaps Varanasi Block) and the claim made by these two districts during the over publicized tenure of my previous boss.

Another problematic state so far static progress of SBM during that period of time was Goa. The political dispensation was positive and also the highest administrative Authority, the Chief Secretary was very much interested to make Goa ODF. My boss made three visits to the state and met from CM to CS, but progress did not move even a single percentage for the next two years. In between my boss sent almost all his favourite officers but no avail. However, by accident, I had to meet some lower level officers on a visit to the state which was not related to progress of ODF directly and understood the real ground problem why Goa could not make any progress in its toilet constructions despite the best intent of the political brass as well as that of the top bureaucratic boss of the state. The lower-level officers who were ordered to construct toilets were never heard (or never tried to hear the problems faced by the lower-level officers of the state) by my boss, who enjoyed the hospitality of the state Government three times before my accidental meeting with the lower-level officers. I dutifully informed the actual problem faced by the Goa Government's officials on the ground after my return to Delhi. The street-smart boss tried to blame me for not informing the problem faced by the Goa Government officials in implementing SBM beforehand. However, with an intriguing smile I replied, 'Sir senior officers of our office had already visited more than 10 times before my visit to the state (I avoided intentionally to tell that out of these 10 visits three were done by my smart boss himself), but could not be able to know the real problem on the ground.'

The smart boss understood from me, what I intended to say. Finally, on my request, he sent the Prerak, from Uttarakhand, working in Tripura to initiate some actions on the ground. With her extreme efforts, both the districts of Goa also declared themselves ODF at the nick of the time and became one of the last states who declared themselves ODF. Unfortunately, the Prerak had to face a lot of harassment in the hands of the State Government officials in clearing her TA bill from Orissa to Goa as they insisted, they would clear her bill only if Department would give a clear instruction to clear the TA bill of the Prerak. Neither Government officials of Goa nor concerned officers sitting at the Department were interested to clear the genuine bill of the Prerak. Finally, I had to write a letter to the Goa Government to clear the bill, and then only she was paid the bill. Thanks to unsympathetic Indian bureaucracy at all levels!

In the flip side, one of the SBM criticizers sent me a photograph showing a person sitting on the railway track for open defecation in UP. I only replied back to him like this, 'I am happy that nowadays only a very few persons are using railway tracks for OD in UP, unlike the pre-SBM period when you would have found hordes of people on the railway track in the entire belt of UP and Bihar.'

As expected, it is a fact that a group of people was sceptical about the implementation of the Mission. Even a famous Hindi poet used to write sarcastic poems for the impending disaster of the Mission. Many people from the opposing groups of the NDA Government who ridiculed the

Prime Minister's speech from the walls of the Red Fort on 15th August 2014, started finding faults in the implementation of the SBM and some of them even doubted the intent. No doubt it was very unfortunate, but the people of India responded to their critiques by declaring themselves ODF on 2nd October 2019.

Considering the vastness of the country and diametrically opposite mindsets of the people due to geographical and social outlook towards any socio-economic issues including the issue of OD, there were not only some issues to be addressed at a different level, but also despite the best efforts, there were some misses and therefore some shots were off the target by a whisker or by miles. These misses, particularly those were missed by miles had been highlighted by the vested interest groups within India and outside India who wanted to demean the efforts of the Government and the common people of India.

To know the ground realities, as already mentioned three consecutive surveys at the behest of the World Bank, popularly known as NARSS were conducted by an independent agency under the supervision of a committee headed by an academician and whose other members of the committee were from different Government and Non-Government organizations. All these three surveys with sample size of more than 90,000 households across the country threw some very important statistics for the SBM and its implementation. The results of these three surveys almost conform to the figures available on the website of MIS (Management Information System) of the Ministry/ Department of Drinking Water and Sanitation.

However, some survey reports conducted by Ministry of Statistics and Programme Implementation through NSSO, Ministry of Health and Family Welfare (through IIPS-Indian Institute of Population Science), including that of two very important Government surveys, viz. NSSO (71st) and NFSH-5 did not support the claims of the Ministry/ Department in respect of a few States though for the majority of the states, the results of these surveys and NARSS are almost the same. Some surveys conducted by some NGOs with very small sample sizes highlighted the brownie points of the Mission. Results of NSOO and NFSH-5 panicked some of the officers of the Department led by my boss whose highly hyped reputation was at a stake. Instead of trying to see the problems on the ground in the right spirit, my boss tried to find fault in the survey methodology with some laughable excuses. These laughable excuses only made the situation further deteriorate to the uneasy situations within the Department. My boss, instead of taking course correction at the field level, tried to control the survey results by dragging the name of the Hon'ble PM at every level. Luckily, those who were looking at the survey reports in the proper perspectives, heaved a sigh of relief once he left the department (many doubt he was actually shunted out honourably from the Department) before he could damage the image of the Hon'ble PM by not allowing the reports to be published in time, dragging the name of the Hon'ble PM sir, though the fact of the matter, it is learned from sources (reliable? cannot be authenticated) Hon'ble PM sir showed anguish for the misleading figures in some of the states.

Now let us discuss in the true spirit, why these misses were there despite of massive public participation and massive efforts from all the Swachhagrais, Sarpanches, village Pradhans, teachers, students, Political Leaders, Religious Leaders, officers, officials, and consultants of the Central Government and all the State Governments.

First of all, the efforts were not uniform in all the levels in all the states/ districts/ blocks/ villages. There were a lot of differences in the level and intensity in efforts in inter and intra geographical units depending upon the background of the people in respect of social, religious, financial status of the people and so on. Inter-state differences could be observed by each and every one who was following the implementation of the Mission. Less number of people was observing the intra-state disparities based on different indicators. As we go down to the lower level of geographical areas, we observed that there were huge differences in mindsets, financial status, and social status among the villagers which effectively misrepresent the ground reality in some of the states where economic disparity was high and caste divide was extremely wide.

The second reason was the difference amongst political leadership. As already shared with the readers that in Tripura, one of the states of North-East whose majority of the populations are living in plains and there was no problem in construction of toilets unlike the other North Eastern States, other than Assam, whose toilet coverage was 74% since 2011 census to 2017 and became 100% coverage much before 2nd October 2019 once political leadership in power was changed in between. However, in most of the South Indian states, there was practically no or minimal impact in the implementation of SBM irrespective of political leadership in power.

The third reason was the difference of mindsets of officers who were in the helm of affairs at state level/ district level. There is a myth that direct recruit officers are having better in mindset in implementation of SBM compared to the officers who are aged being non-direct recruit officers. According to me, this might be a well-cultivated myth by the media and by the direct recruit officers themselves because of their better relation with the media due to better communication skills, particularly communication skills in English of these officers. Am I throwing a stone to a hornet's nest? My experience on my visits to different districts in Assam and other states might be the basis of my claim on this particular issue. In other words, my observations might be limited to the implementation of the SBM scheme, not for other schemes or other activities looked after by the DMs/ DCs as parts of their mandated duties.

Local politics also played an important role in the misses. The people who supported the winning candidate in the last Panchayat election used to get priority over the opposing people, even though the instruction was very clear that all the eligible beneficiaries would get Government incentive to construct their toilets. However, on ground it was observed that some of the areas of some villages were systematically kept out of coverage in providing all the beneficiary schemes including that of incentive money for toilet constructions. I had a very interesting experience in Tripura. A retired teacher from Central School had a magnificent toilet complex constructed at a cost of Rs. Two

Lakh. However, he was also a SBM beneficiary of incentive money of Rs.12,000/-. Another family having already three toilets were also a SBM beneficiary of incentive money of Rs.12,000/-. On the other hand, in the same locality, some poor families were not given any incentive money from the Government. Later on, the concern Tata Prerak told me that the practice of releasing incentive money to the rich and depriving the poor people was very common in Tripura. According to them, to get Government benefits one must be a supporter of a particular party during the previous regime when toilet coverage was not improving at all. Though I could not be able to verify the veracity of the statement made by the Tata Preraks, I myself found the experience of releasing incentive money to the rich people and depriving poor people at least in two villages which were not very far from the state capital, Agartala. After visiting few more villages across the state in different districts, I understood the reason of the stagnation in progress of the coverage of toilets for more than six years in Tripura.

Another very interesting complaint I got when I had visited Dibrugarh District of Assam in the summer season of 2018. The village was hardly 25 KM from Dibrugarh city when a widow complained me that the quality of the toilet constructed by the PHE department was very bad and her toilet was completely damaged within six months after its construction. The officials accompanying me became little bit uncomfortable at the accusation of the widow, naturally. To find the veracity of the complaint, when I wanted to see the toilet, to my utter dismay, I observed that the toilet was constructed at the lowermost part of her large compound and all rainwater was deposited in that particular area. Naturally, I understood very clearly, no matter the quality of the construction of the toilet might had been, there was every chance that the toilet had to be damaged. I asked the widow, why she had allotted that particular place for construction of the toilet. As expectedly, she did not have a proper answer to my pointed question. However, I was reported by the concerned engineer that the toilet of the widow was reconstructed afterwards just to make the widow happy. I thought that might not be a 'one off case' of non-cooperation of the beneficiaries to the implementing department. In another village of Assam, I got complaint from the NGO who was constructing the toilets on behalf of the PHE department that some of the beneficiaries used to take away or hide the construction materials for use of some other purposes causing lot of difficulties for the NGOs in construction of the allotted toilets for the beneficiaries.

Though I was not involved to look after the progress of that particular state, I came to know that, apparently a wrong decision on payment of incentive money by a particular state had de-motivated the common likely beneficiaries to construct toilets. In that particular state, the state government had decided to release the incentive money only when the whole village (later on whole ward) would be declared ODF. This particular idea was borrowed from a decision taken by a young and dynamic Deputy Commissioner of Karnal district of Haryana where most of villagers were rich who can afford to construct the toilets of their own. This innovative decision helped the district become ODF much before the other districts of the state could become ODF. But when this decision was taken by that particular state, they perhaps forgot that historically a good number of the poor people of India unfortunately reside in that particular state. This decision was continued till the end of December, 2018 despite repeated requests were made by the Central Ministry to change the decision of the state. Though this state claimed to become ODF by October, 2019, survey reports of both NSS and NHFS-5 showed much below toilet coverage on the ground. My boss who was very particular in building his own image, did not dare to ask those officers looking after the progress of that particular state along with some other defaulting states or those officers of those states who were responsible for implementing the scheme on ground how and why toilet coverage in those states was so low.

However, he tried to find faults in survey methodology of these two surveys and put pressure not to publish those reports knowing fully well that the survey results were in conformity with the ground reality so far toilet coverage was concerned as he made several personal visits along with some of his blue-eyed consultants to feel the heat of the ground reality of those states. Contradicting his own arguments, he advised these states to submit additional lists of beneficiaries with the new nomenclature, 'out of base line' and after few months more additional lists with another artistic name of those lists of beneficiaries, 'No one left behind.' I was cent percent sure had he continued, he would have approved another type of lists with another beautiful name with the help of his super intelligent 'air force' and few extra-ordinary manipulative consultants (no officer of the Ministry/ Department was in his decision-making core group who left the Ministry two –three days before his exit from the department). Being a statistician, I was surprised to see how every time adding a new type of lists of beneficiaries with few lakhs (sometimes more than even 10 lakhs) in these states, their percentage of coverage of access to toilets could not go up beyond 100% as claimed by those states and finding fault in statistical methodology by the core group of people in the Department at the behest of that particular self-glorified officer. I was often targeted for the shortfall in coverage of toilets in these states but he never allowed me to visit these states to know the ground reality.

Sometimes, some super intelligent people do not use their common senses or try to ignore a message which might be 'writing on the wall' for their own vested interest. My very intelligent boss might have thought everyone was fool to understand many things on the ground and tried his best to misguide even the highest authority also with some inflated figures which was not believed by the highest authority, as expected, to the utter frustration of my boss. On his instructions, another group of vested interest consultants twisted some definitions on coverage of toilets to inflate the toilet coverage figures in some of the select states and try to defend the coverage figures by writing some articles in some newspapers with absurd justifications. Instead of pulling up those inefficient officers for whom the progress was not good my boss tried to fudge statistics putting gun on the head of the statisticians. Luckily for the country, perhaps the highest authority also came to know about the unethical steps taken by the officer and probably that was the reason why he had left or he was unceremoniously shunted out of the department, as doubted by many. I think that at present, the department is sincerely trying to fill the gaps between the reported figures and the actual coverage of toilets on ground without trying to garner any accolades from anywhere though some moles planted by earlier boss is trying to sabotage the efforts of the department.

Luckily, for the country those 'misses' are to be made another undisputed 'hits' by the present dispensation of the Government though the highest Authority remains the same as his intent was very clear, India should be neat and clean like any other developed countries of the world.

I have the last laugh when NFHS-5 results came to the public domain, when toilet coverage in the entire NE (which was monitored by me), individually or collectively came out to be more than 90% and whereas the states looked after by my boss directly with the tacit help and support from his 'so called most efficient team of officers and consultants' came out be below 70% toilet coverage. But who cares for me! After all, I cannot speak English so fluently with lot of jargons like my boss. Same is the case of his air force team. Therefore, my boss and his team got accolades and I was left high and dry as non-grata for the Department as usual. My boss and his team of officers used to claim that the survey teams engaged in these states were inefficient and the informants of these states are not truthful (short of claiming that they were liars) about having toilets and that is why toilet coverage in these states came out so low. Is anybody other than his coterie in this world, believing the claim of my boss on that account? At least, I am not convinced about the claim of my boss.

However, one should understand and fair to my boss that earlier also toilet coverage in these states was very low compared to the toilet coverage in the North Eastern States of India.

'Water, Water, Water is everywhere, but not a single drop to drink.' It was a famous dialogue of Napoleon (obviously he was not saying in English, I am only translating it from French to English keeping the intrinsic meaning of the sentence) when the warship he was travelling lost its way in the sea and sailors were thirsty but there was no sufficient potable water in the ship to drink. The same problem would be facing by any person if he has to be stuck in the middle of flood water where despite being in the midst of water, he cannot consume flood water due to obvious reasons.

However, problem in India, so far drinking water is concerned, much more complicated than the example given above. In our country, more than 4500 villages are having ground water contamination of Arsenic and other poisonous minerals as on today. More than 250 districts out of 700 plus districts are water scarce and many are joining the list on a super-fast speed. The rain God must have been guided by a stupid statistician who believes in average, not in dispersion. I understand the earlier sentence may not be easily understandable by the non-statisticians. Let me try to explain it in a layman's language. Average is a common measure for an indicator, in this case, rain fall in a particular month in a particular place. Take for example average rainfall in Delhi in the month of September for the last hundred years is 200 mm (not exactly). Now in the month of September, 2021, in the first three days of September had actually crossed the average rainfall of September for the last hundred years. As a result of that Delhi faced a flood like situation without much improvement in the level of ground water or any other benefits for the residents of Delhi. Unfortunately, it is not a 'one-off' example of getting non-uniform rainfall in a month or in a rainy season in Delhi. Unfortunately, it is not the story of one place or one state or one country only, but also, it is a normal and horrifying story of the whole world. As a result of the erratic rainfall, humanity and environment are facing lot of problems including shortage of potable water for men and animals. On the other hand, irregular rainfall gives the whole world draught and flood both simultaneously in the same geographical and political entity.

To compound the water scarcity problems in India, coverage of piped water supply at household level was barely 11% before the implementation of JJM (Jal Jeevan Mission) in India. In some states, like in Assam, it was as low as 1.76% only on 15th August 2019 despite not being Assam a water scarce state.

Then the epoch-making announcement (universal pipe water supply) came from our beloved PM Sir from the walls of the Red Fort on 15.08.2019 once again like he did on 15.08.2014 for providing IHHL to all the eligible households of India. In his 'Independence Day' speech, he declared that all the households of India will be provided with tap water connection by December, 2024. It is also nothing sort of a herculean task as the department has to facilitate the State and Union Territory Governments to provide functional household tap water connections to almost fifteen crore households in five years' time. In other words, on the average three crore functional household tap water connections in a year have to be provided by the government. But it is only a rough statistical calculation. To achieve this mammoth target within target time, lot of planning at all levels, arrangement of huge finance, finding water sources for water supply on sustainable basis at least for the next fifty-odd years and so on are the pre-requisites. Even procurement of raw materials like pipes, water lifting machines of different capacity may be a challenge for many states and Union Territories with varied degree of difficulties. The topography of the country is a challenge for identifying water sources and construction of different types of reservoirs for water supply depending upon topography the of the places, even within the same state/ UT. And there the vision of a leader plays the most important role to visualize the problem properly and distribute of duties to the persons available in the system who have the capacity to drive to vision of the leader. As a result of that thinking process, best possible human resources were posted in the Department of Drinking Water and Sanitation (also may have gotten rid of few officers) to implement JJM in the true spirit.

The scheme had started with a modest beginning in 2019 and unfortunately, all of us had to stumble upon something after few months of its roll-out which nobody had anticipated in the beginning of even 2020.

The menace of Covid-19 arrived in India in the early part of 2020 like a hurricane destroying everything on its way. With a slow start, Covid-19 engulfed the entire country with varying degree of intensity.

Once the menace of the first phase of Covid lost its tempo, with the cooperation of the mass people of the country and the direction of the leadership, the construction of the drinking water projects and laying of pipelines to the premises of the rural households regained the momentum to the delight of everyone concerned. However, again, the second wave of Covid-19 made another road block in the implementation of JJM in almost all the states and UTs

It is worth mentioning that during the implementation of earlier scheme, NRWP (National Rural Water Project) every time a new Government comes into power or a new public representative was elected, a few new projects for pipe water connections were started on paper and in some occasion foundation stone were also erected; but none had cared for completion of those projects. In 2018-19, the number of incomplete projects stood around 2 lakhs in the entire country of which hardly 10% of projects had completed their works more than 75%. A good number of projects were not even started or only 10% of works had been completed. Further one internal survey under my supervision found that a good number of projects were not found on the ground, but shown as functional by the concerned state governments. Though the diluted report was shared with the states, it is not known to me whether any action was initiated or not against the concerned persons for uploading such misinformation in the web portal of the Ministry? Further, even from the survey it was not known whether the discrepancies were limited to uploading of faulty data due to misclassification or those were uploaded with malafide intention. As the Ministry of Drinking Water and Sanitation was not in a position to initiate any action due to the federal structure in the country where water supply is basically a state subject.

However, to streamline the implementation of NRDWM and sort out those discrepancies, the Department of Drinking Water and Sanitation had initially prioritized in releasing Central share for those projects which were completed more than 75% of their ground works. Unfortunately, in some states including that of North Eastern states, not a single project was in that stage. Finally, having no alternative, even for the 25% completed projects; a Central share was released for many states.

However, once JJM was launched everything had been changed for all practical purposes on the ground.

The broad objectives of the JJM can be summarised like this:

1. All the stakeholders are determined to provide FHTC (Functional Household Tap Water Connection) to every rural household;

2. To prioritize the provision of FHTCs in quality-affected areas, villages in drought-prone and desert areas, aspirational districts, Sansad Adarsh Gram Yojna (SAGY) villages, etc. necessary plan will be drawn up.

3. To provide functional tap connection to Schools, Anganwadi centres, Dhramshalas, GP buildings, Health centres, wellness centres, and community buildings on priority all stakeholders are impressed upon.

4. The Ministry and concerned departments will take appropriate steps to develop a monitoring system to see the functionality of tap connections.

5. To promote and ensure voluntary ownership among the local community by way of contribution in cash, kind and/ or labour, and voluntary labour (shramdaan) the mass people will be encouraged.

6. To assist in ensuring the sustainability of the water supply system, i.e. water source, water supply infrastructure, and funds for regular O&M will be arranged seamlessly.

7. To empower and develop human resources in the sector such that the demands of construction, plumbing, electrical, water quality management, water treatment, catchment protection, O&M, etc. are taken care of in short and long-term basis.

8. To bring awareness on various aspects and significance of safe drinking water and involvement of stakeholders in manner that make water everyone's business, appropriate steps will be taken.

As Jal Jeevan Mission is a time-bound programme, to monitor the progress of the mission, during my time, an Integrated Management Information System (IMIS) portal has been developed to capture the year-wise and state-wise physical progress of the Mission along with fund utilization status, up to the village level. The portal also displays information about water-quality testing laboratories up to the sub-division level and the number of tests conducted in these laboratories. The portal is updated on real time basis.

In a nutshell, water being a State subject, this Department of Government of India provides financial and technical assistance to the State Governments/ UT Administrations for providing water supply to the rural population. A Citizen Charter has also been formulated accordingly. A provision has been made for constant feedback and suggestion from the recipients and stakeholders regarding delivery of services. It is hoped constant feedback from the stakeholders will help in enabling the department to improve the service delivery mechanism and make DDWS more response to the needs of the citizen of the country.

As a part of my duties, to see the progress of JJM and SBM plus, I visited Nagaland during December, 2021. This visit was very important for me as despite of resistance from my well-wishers, I visited Nagaland just 3 days after the firing incident of Assam Rifles on civilians in Mon District of Nagaland (on 4th December and I made my journey from 7th December in the state). As per the approved programme I reached Dimapur airport three hours late of scheduled time; thanks to mismanagement of the concerned airlines at Kolkata airport. As a result of that I missed my lunch and directly went to a village of New Land Area of Dimapur, around 40 KM from the airport. The road leading to the village is un-enviable with lot of large pot holes and took almost two hours to reach the village.

When I reached the village, the village was completely submerged into pitched dark though it was only half past five in the evening. A large number of people were waiting for me and after meeting the people I forgot the painful journey to reach the village. Further, their hospitably showed their love for me as a representative of Government of India during a period when the National Media and local media were very vocal about the unfortunate firing incident in Mon District.

Though it was pitched dark, it was not difficult for me to understand the village was indeed a very neat and clean visit. Though the village was not marked as ODF plus village, the village was proud of having hundred percent IHHL coverage, having a community toilet complex and having every household a soak pit for grey water management as reported by the village headman and the villagers present during my visit. Further, each and every household was provided functional tap water connection.

In the early morning of the next day, I proceeded to Zunheboto district which was located about 250 km from Dimapur. Those who have experience in travelling through the Hilly terrain of North Eastern part of India know that distance of 250 KM is a very long distance in the hilly tract. A message had come to the driver while we were crossing Kohima town; that as the short road was not in a good condition, we should take the long route. While travelling by the better road, with lot of irritation in my voice, I asked my driver, 'if this is the better road, what is the condition of the other road?' Instead of giving an answer, he laughed loudly. His laugh forced me also to laugh looking at the plight of myself.

Without saying one can understand that each and every bone of mine was cracking whenever the driver was negotiating a pot hole. Before reaching Zunheboto, the escort officer told me that we had to visit a village to see implementation of JJM. Though each and every bone of mine was crying with unbearable pain, I uttered 'yes, I would like to see the village.'

It was a village which was located some 10 km from the main road. As it was already 7 PM, it was like travelling in a hilly track in the midnight. However, when I reached the village, I became very happy to see the people and their enthusiasm in their faces to meet me. After taking much needed a cup of tea and biscuit I went around the village and asked the local engineer few routine questions like, whether water supplied to the villagers with 'gravitational method', whether last household is getting sufficient water or not, whether the water supply scheme was in operation before JJM was launched, is there any contamination in the water supplied. Further, I asked a few of the villagers, 'what is change in the life of the villagers when water is supplied at their premises etc.'

I thanked the Almighty to give me an opportunity to meet these people of remote areas of Nagaland and proceeded to the district HQs where my night stay was arranged.

The guest house where my stay was arranged was a nice guest house owned by an Ex-Minister of Nagaland. The guest house was maintained by the family of his second son. After taking a beautiful homemade dinner, I forgot the 'more than 12 hours' horrible journey' to reach Zunheboto.

On the next day also, I visited three more villages in the Zunheboto district. The receptions in every village made me so happy that my old cracking bones also began to dance with pure joy and happiness.

Many people ask me why I used to visit a good number of villages in each and every tour I made to a State/ UT knowing fully well that the villages which were selected for my visit were the best ones in terms of implementation of SBM and JJM. My answer on this pinpointed question is, 'since I visit more villages in every tour to a state compared to my other senior colleagues, the number of villages became more where implementation of SBM and JJM is better compared to the states where my senior colleagues use to visit the consuming same number of days in those states.'

On my next tour, I visited some of the villages of Assam and Meghalaya. In Assam, there are some large multi-village schemes covering as many as 200-300 villages alongwith thousands of single village schemes. In Assam, in most of the single village schemes, ground water has been pumped to the water tank from which water is distributed to the villagers without any treatment. On the other hand, in large schemes, surface water, mostly from the perennial rivers is pumped to large treatment plants. After, treating the water, making free from any contamination, water has been distributed to the households in many villages simultaneously. As the rivers are of perennial nature in Assam, these water sources likely to be sources for the next forty-fifty years without much difficulty. However, the single village schemes will likely to have problems of contaminations and drying up water source in near future which Government of Assam has to guard. No doubt, for the time being, these schemes will serve the purpose of providing functional tape water connection to all the rural households in Assam.

Unlike Nagaland, roads maintained by Central Government and State Government in Meghalaya are very good and therefore, I was able to visit as many as 8 villages in a single day to see the implementation of JJM in the villages of Meghalaya. However, like Nagaland, in Meghalaya also most of the schemes are gravity based and mostly these schemes are single village scheme. Like Nagaland, almost all the household are getting per capita more than 100 litres water daily which is much above recommended per capita water availability of 55 litres per day. It is feared, over use of water from water sources may lead to drying up of the sources. However, good thing in both the states are that the grey water harvesting using soak pits at household level on 'cent percent basis' have been implemented in true spirit.

My last official tour to see progress of ODF plus including safe disposal of plastics, Govardhan and JJM was my hurricane 4 day visit to Assam and Arunachal Pradesh. As already stated, implementation of JJM and SBM plus are extremely good in Arunachal Pradesh and of late Assam is also peaking up.

Through all my official visits to different states, I am sure the targets of ODF plus will take few more years as it is a very complicated issue; but providing safe water through functional household tap water connection (FHTC) under JJM will be achieved within the target time, December, 2024. (The whole chapter is written in my own perspective only and is nothing official about it)

Chapter XII: Incomplete Journey of My Life?

No man in this world is successful in all the categories in life as a son, as a son in law, as a brother, brother-in-law, as a husband, as a relative, as a father, as a friend, as an officer, as an employee, as a boss, as a subordinate, as a professional whatever he pursues, as a sportsman and even as a normal human being. Similarly, no lady in this world can be successful in all the fields as a counterpart of a man (as a daughter, as a daughter in law and so on), in the fields as mentioned above. However, other way round, you may find many in this world who were not successful even in a single parameter mentioned above. So far, I am concerned, I am somewhat a successful person as a son, as a son in law, as a husband, and as a father, perhaps. So, what is the harm in standing in the midst of the majority and enjoy life! Further, one should understand and remember that success is a relative word in the real world.

As an old man of sixty plus, looking back to my life as a child, as a student at different level, as an officer and as a writer, I have no regret for my achievements. I have digested each and every humiliation in my life as a new experience in my life and went ahead in my life with new vigour. I am thankful to the Almighty to choose me as a person who can withstand all the humiliation in life and look forward for a new sunrise with a new beginning.

Further, I want to finish the book with a story which suggests that this book should be read by them only who think that I am somewhat a successful person in my life.

A small-time businessman was bringing Multani clay from Kabul to Delhi on his shoulders in two sacks using a carry-pole. Fortunately, before he could cross Thar Desert, he was able to sell one sack of Multani clay. To make equal weight on both sides of the pole, he decided to fill the empty bag with desert sand. While he was filling the sack, a man coming from the opposite side asked the hard working but small-time businessman what he was doing. When the businessman told exactly what he was doing, after a hearty laugh, the stranger suggested the businessman, 'you could have divided the

Multani clay into two equal parts which would have reduced your burden and also you will be able to move faster in the desert.'

The businessman asked the stranger, 'before I take a decision on your advice, will you tell me, who are you and from where you are coming from?'

The stranger introduced himself to the stranger with a tired and depressed voice, 'I am an unemployed person and went to Delhi to try my luck to get some good employment. Unfortunately, I could not find any and therefore I am returning from Delhi to my village.'

Hearing the answer from the stranger, the businessman smiled and told the stranger, 'Your advice may have some justification. But sorry, my friend, I never take any advice from an unsuccessful person.'

The stranger left the place with a remark, 'Days have gone, when there were takers of good advices.'

The businessman however, did not say anything and filled the empty sack with desert-sand and started his journey towards Delhi.

After few days of tiring journey, the businessman reached the border of Delhi. He was accosted by some soldiers and asked the businessman what was in his sacks. When he told about sacksful of desert sand in one sack and Multani clay in the other one, he was immediately taken to the higher officer.

His fear turned out to be a joyful moment when he was told by the Kotowal (head of the sentry gate) that Sultan was sending them to the desert for a sack full of desert sand to get treatment on his backpain as advised by the royal doctor. Without mincing much words, his sand was purchased with 100 gold coins by the officer as the officer and his soldiers did not need to make a tiresome journey to the desert to collect desert-sand. Another 10 gold coins were given in lieu of the sack full of Multani sand. Thus, he got 20 gold coins for the Multani clay and 100 gold coins for the sack full of desert-sand.

While returning back to his hometown, the businessman filled his sacks with goods which were easily available in the markets of Delhi, but were very scarce in his home town.

Moral of the story:

Best advices are always coming from the unsuccessful persons who could not use those for their own good. Therefore, one should go by his own instincts and take advice only from successful persons even if those may appear to be impractical advices at the first place.

However, we should always remember that we all are 'the businessman' and at the same time, we all are 'the failed stranger' of the above story, in one field or the other.

I finish my incomplete journey of life here itself with a hope that one day I shall be successful in life and some people will take my advice also in the right spirit.

Annexure-I

Photographs Of Some Of The Persons Who Have (Had) Infused Positive Energy In Me Throughout My Life

So far the photo of my face inside a donkey may have two intrinsic meanings: 1. Donkey is a very intelligent animal, but always the word 'Donkey (Gadha) is referred to mean a dumb person. 2. Donkey is a very hard working animal.

MY MOTHER DASHAMI BORAH

Main Stay In My Life

(From L to R) Standing: Monalisha (wife), Minakshi (sister) and Urbashi (Sister in law)

Sitting: Anusuya (daughter on my lap), Bharat Chandra Borah (Father), Ayusman (On my father's lap), Mother and Dr. Apurba Borah (Elder Brother)

Above: Apurba Krishna Buragohain (Brother in Law)

Mrs. Monalisha (My Life Partner), a brave lady who always stood by my side during all the tempests of life in our long 36 plus years of married life

Monalisha (In school uniform)

Miss Anusuya (Elder Daughter): A successful young lady on her own right, who made me a proud father many years ago

Mr. Ayusman Vikramjeet (Son): A young man of independent thoughts and spirits; who is also a good painter.

Miss Anwesha (Younger Daughter): She is a soft looking tough girl. She is always ready to fight for a right cause.

Ayusman, Monalisha and Anwesha at Kovalam Beach

Me and My wife when we were not fighting

Dr. D. P. Phukan (Father in Law), Monalisha, Mrs. T. Phukan (Mother in Law), Anusuya and Ayusman

Mr. Bhaskar (a senior officer of Government of Assam) and Mrs. Alee Phukan (brother in Law and Sister In law)

(From Lto R) Me, My Wife, Dr. Swapna Gogoi (sister in law) Dr. Simanta Gogoi (brother in Law) and Mrs. T. Phukan (MIL)

Late P. Barpatra (Uncle of my wife with my elder daughter was seen on his lap) alongwith some memorable pictures in India and around the World

Some memorable pictures in India and around the World

Some memorable family pictures alongwith picture of Mr. Surajit Barua

Some memorable pictures in India and around the World

With my wife, Dr. KK Nath, Mrs. Julie Nath (A sister without blood relation) and their children in a family GTG

Another sister, Mrs. Swapnali and her ever smiling husband, Avinash

Anwesha, Hiya, Amrin and I were standing with 'Pragya' team. It is a telefilm based on my mother's childhood, written by me.

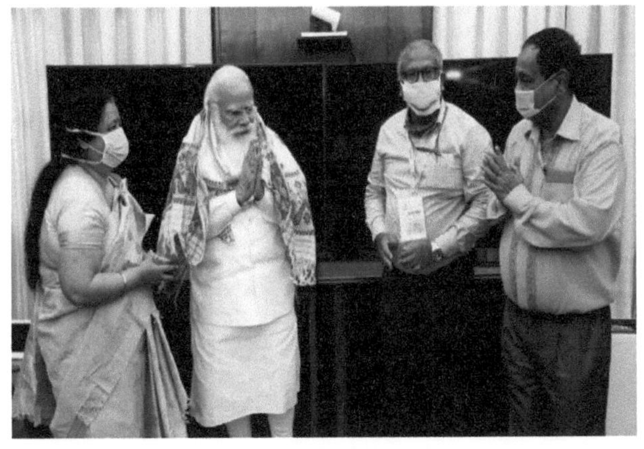

Without any doubt, this is the most 'Iconic Photo' of our family taken in the PMO office situated at Parliament (Sansad Bhawn) of India at 12-00 Noon on 16.03.2021.

(From Left to Right): My wife, PM Sir, Me and Mr. Atanu Saikia

MULA GABHARU

Two Proud Moments for me when Dr. Himanta Biswa Sarma, the Hon'ble CM of Assam had been seen flaunting a copy of my book, 'Mula Gabharu: A story of Valour and Patriotism' and a copy of my book, Chandraprabha: The Iron Lady of Assam (In presence of DD Guwahati Officials). Courtesy to: Mr. Ankur Kalita and Mr. Atanu Saikia

Two Proud Moments when Shri Gajendra Singh Shekhawat, the Union Cabinet Minister of Jal Shakti posed with my books, 'Blessed One', 'Chandraprabha: The Iron Lady of Assam', 'Blessed One Part II' and 'Mula Gabharu: A story of Extreme Valour and Patriotism' in two different occasions

My Book was flaunted by the Deputy Speaker of Rajya Sabha, Shri Bhubaneswar Kalita. Courtesy to: Mr. Atanu Saikia

A screen shot of a tweeter message from Ms. Kara Skinner, an American Critique

Recognition by another Department as a team leader

**The Friends Who Stood By Me
During My Thick and Thins**

**From L to R (Top Row) Diganta Sharma, Rana Bhuya, Sanjib Gohain Barua, Pradeep De, Naresh Sharma
(Bottom Line) M.M. Hasija, Sanjay, Ramesh Aggarwal, Surajit Barua and Ratna Jena (Rakhi Sister).
Not in Picture: Haresswar Hazarika, Pradip Saloi, Dr. Pradip Somani, Dr. Bhaba Bora, Richa Shankar, Samir Sinha, Kajol Jain, Dipetendra Mohan Das, Arropjyoti Das, Shanti Narayan Deka and some of my childhood friends and some relatives.**

Names and Photographs are not in any particular order

There are many friends of mine like Shri SL Mineria, Shri Ghanshyam and the junior ISS officers like Shri Chadradeep Jha and Shri Kamal Pandey who stood by me during my trying times, all of whose names are not mentioned here; but I am always grateful to all of them.

Dr. Bharat Lalji and Dr. Yugal Joshiji have lot of contributions for career upswing as a writer

Few Early Motivators of mine as Writer: (Clockwise): Anuja, Rima and Bordoloi, Mishraji and Poli

Ms. Avneet Kaur (Spiritual Daughter), has been a pillar of Strength in my life since she had joined as a young officer in our office in 2014.She had also uploaded my first book on Smashwords platform

Ms. Deepika Verma (Spiritual Daughter), has been another solid pillar of strength since I met her in 2012. She had helped me in naming my first ebook, Random Thoughts Through a Coloured Prism

Miss Jahnabi Hazarika (My Lucky Charm and Cover-page Girl of many of my books) and who always stood by me since we met dramatically on 13.05.2018 due to a storm over IGI Airport and the flight was diverted to Jaipur. Incidentally in my imagination, she epitomised the ultimate beauty of an Assamese Rural Girl who struggled to be afloat in a Mega City, much before we met on that fateful day. Fortunately, she was found to be more beautiful by heart than her beautiful face. I always pray to God, she should be successful in her life, but always remain beautiful by heart.

Another daughter of mine without blood relation,
Ms. Reena Nagar

Three Young ladies, very close to my heart: Ms. Pinky Pathak, Ms. Jahnabi Hazarika and Ms. Amrin Sultana

There are few

(Clockwise) Yamini (Rajashthan/ WB), Dimi (Assamese), Siriesha (Andhra Pradesh), Isha (Jahrkhand), Philamajan (Manipur), Upasana (Uttarakhand) Kiruthika (Tamil Nadu) not in picture. One Common thing: All are close to me(No particular order is followed)

There are few more young ladies across the country with whom I have very good relation based on mutual trust and respect for each other.

Three young ladies who prefer to fight with me on slightest pretext which I always adore.

Thanks to IA's mismanagement for which I missed my connecting flight from Kolkata to New Delhi, I met the new Icon of Assam, Lovleena Borgohain at IGI

The photograph was clicked during the inauguration function of my book, 'Blessed One Part-II' at CSOI. Other than me and my three favourite young ladies, Ram Pratap, a dashing ISS officer is seen in the picture.

A still of the Hindi serial 'Aparajita' aired by DD Kisan, based on my story, 'Aparajeeta'.

Another Iconic Photo of my life. Can you see me?

For me, he is like Dronacharya to Ekalabya so far poetry is concerned, who does not know that he has a student in me

The Dark man is seen with my favourite actor Mr. Akshaya Kumar

These are the magnificent people who have helped me in both official and unofficial works during my posting in the DDWS from 2016 to 2022. Alongwith me (From L to R): Mr. RK Maurya, Mr.S. Murmu, Mr.MK Gupta, Mr.Dharamvir, Mr. Dharmender Kumar, Mr. VM Rana, Mr. Ashish, Mr. Anil, Ms.Mandira, Dr. RK Bhutani and Mr. S.S. Arora (Shri Rambali Mishra is not in the picture)

Along with me, (R to L) Sudhir Kumar Sinha, Mohan Kumar, Dharmbir, Bheem Singh Meena, Santosh Kumar Mishra, Deepak Dagar, Pratap Soreng, Kartik Singhal, Ashish Singh Bounal

NIC Team: (L to R) Shiv Kumar, Pradeep Saxena, Shri Surya Mohan Srivastava, Smt. Seemantinee Sengupta, D.C. Misra. (OP Aggarwal, Nitish, Pradeep, Rajesh, Saif and Jayonto are not in the picture)

It is an Instagram Status of an unknown person where my book is shown. Courtesy to Mr. Ankur Kalita

A Photograph away from Government Duties was taken on the 147th Birthday of Freedom Fighter Birsa Munda. Courtesy to Mr. D. Chouhan

It is a small recognition as an English writer by Bluerose Publishers

nation 02

Blessings win over curses in 'The Blessed One'

PNS ■ DEHRADUN

Those who are fond of mythological tales will like what Hiranya Borah is doing with the characters in "The Blessed One". The novel revolves around a curse; similar to stories of a condemnation hunting a family generation after generation, the protagonist being on the firing cord of the curse is saved by the blessing of his mother and mother goddess.

The basic theme of the book is "blessings are more powerful than the curses". For someone who has interest in mythology, this book tells the stories of curses, blessings, deception, devotion and fruition.

The story has crisp and smooth twists and every chapter has something different to offer. In his novel, Borah has complete control over the story and style.

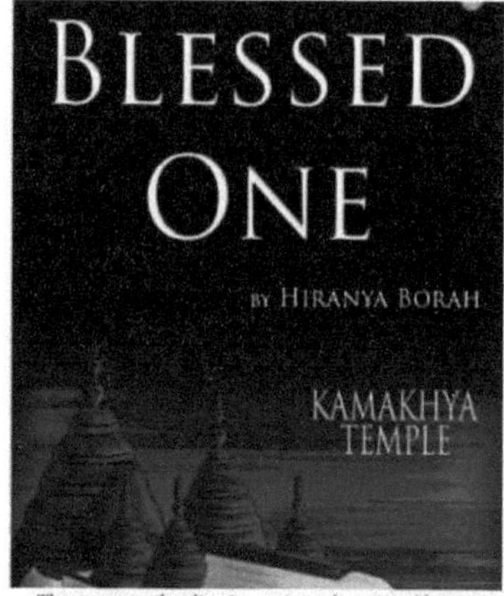

The unexpected ending is a fitting denouement to an epic and memorable excursion.

I was extremely happy to see this news item on my book, 'Blessed One'.

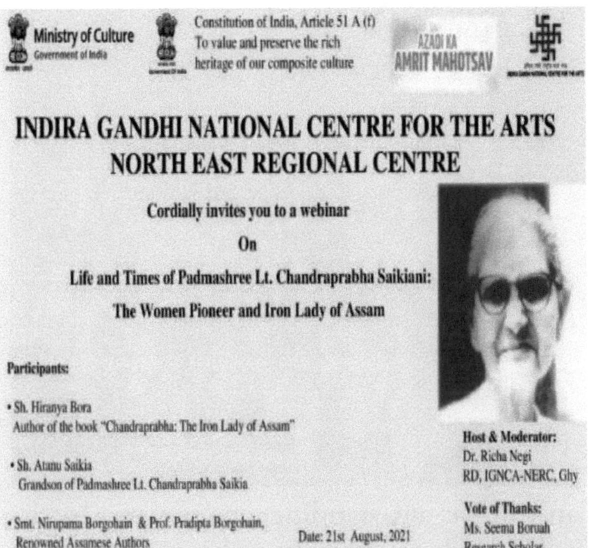

Sometimes, I am also invited to deliver lecture by others.

Can you see me, standing amongst two batches of ISS probationers after delivering my last lecture on SBM and JJM alongwith a long motivational lecture in March, 2022 as a serving officer?

I had a very sentimental moment when Hon'ble Union Minister, Shri Gajendra Singh Shekhawatji was felicitating me on my retirement at a dinner party hosted by him at his residence

My wife and me with the family of Hon'ble Union Minister, Shri Gajendra Singh Shekhawatji on my retirement at a dinner party hosted by him at his residence

My Incomplete Journey: As a son of a village school teacher, I was ready to go to Nehru Place, New Delhi to repair my laptop by taking metro ride on the 11th day of my retirement. The oil painting on the background is a creation of my son.

Annexure-II

Since The Entire List Of Orders Of GOI Is Very Long And Therefore, I Am Attaching Only A Miniscule Of The List Non- Sensitive Important Orders To Show That Despite Showing Faith In Me By Different Departments/ Organisations/ Ministries By Allotting Many Assignment Beyond Statistical Works, I Was Stigmatised As A Bad Officer By My Own Cadre Where Mostly My Own Service Colleagues Were Holding Post Which Were Detrimental In Spoiling My Service Career.

SUPREME COURT OF INDIA

OFFICE ORDER NO. 8/SG/NCMS/2013

JUNE 04, 2013

Ref: Office Order No. 4/SG/NCMS/2012 dated 02.05.2012 of Secretary General, Supreme Court of India.

Hon'ble The Chief Justice of India, by Order dated 30/04/2013 has been pleased to nominate Shri H. Borah, Deputy Director General, Social Statistics Division, Central Statistics Office, Ministry of Statistics and Programme Implementation, Govt. of India, as a member of the NCMS Committee.

4.6.13
(Ravindra Maithani)
Secretary General

Perhaps, this order is the most important order in my opinion as I was appointed as the only technical Officer for this Committee from the Government of India. I had the privilege to continue as the member of the Committee till July, 2016.

[illegible] Bharat Mission (Grameen)

4th Floor, Pt. Deendayal Antyodaya Bhawan,
CGO Complex, Lodhi Road,
New Delhi – 110003
Dated: [illegible]

Office Order

Subject: Composition of Internal Evaluation Committee (IEC) for screening of applications for the Grand Challenge on Sanitation -reg.

In order to carry out the screening of the applications received by the Start-ups for the Grand Challenge for sanitation, an Internal Evaluation Committee (IEC) comprising the following is constituted:

Composition of the Internal Evaluation Committee	
Mr. Hiranya Borah, DDG, DDWS	Chairperson
Mr. Kapil Chaudhary, Director, DDWS	Coordinator
Dr. Anupama, Director, DDWS	Member
Mr. Karanjeet, Jt. Director, DDWS	Member
Mr. Rajeev Jauhari, Deputy Secretary, DDWS	Member
Mr. Uday Narayan Sinha, Deputy Secretary, DDWS	Member
Representative of PSA committee	Member
Representative of MoHUA	Member
Representative of DPIIT	Member
Representative of MyGov	Member

2. This issues with the approval of Secretary, DDWS.

(Magan Lal)
US, SBM-II
Ph No: 011-[illegible]
E-mail: magan.lal@[illegible]

To:

1. All members of IEC
2. Sr. PPS to Secy, DDWS
3. Sr. PPS to AS, DDWS

No. [illegible] **CONFIDENTIAL**

Government of India
Ministry of Electronics and Information Technology
National Informatics Centre
A-Block, CGO Complex, Lodi Road, New Delhi – 110 003

[illegible] February, 2022

OFFICE MEMORANDUM

Subject: **Meeting of Level-2 (External) Assessment Board for review promotion of Group 'A' S&T Officers due as on January 2018, January 2019, July 2020 and January 2021 under the provisions of Personnel Policy and Practice issued by Ministry of Electronics and Information Technology (MeitY) vide Office Memorandum No. 2(11)/2016-Pers.III dated 19.09.2016 – reg.**

The National Informatics Centre is in the process of conducting review promotion of Group 'A' S&T Officers for promotion from the grade of **Scientist-E to Scientist-F**, Pay Matrix-13-A (Rs. 131100-216600). The composition of the Level-2 (External) Assessment Board, duly approved by the competent authority is as given below:

1. Prof. M.N. Doja — Chairman
   Director
   IIIT Sonepat
   Haryana

2. Shri Hiranya Borah — Member
   DDG
   Ministry of Drinking Water and Sanitation
   New Delhi

3. Dr. (Smt) Arvinder Kaur, Prof. Computer Science — Member
   Guru Gobind Singh Indraprastha University
   Delhi

4. Shri Suresh P. Nambiar — Member
   General Manager (Information Systems)
   Indian Oil Corporation Limited

5. Shri G. Mayil Muthu Kumaran — Member
   Scientist-G
   National Informatics Centre
   New Delhi

The meeting of Level-2 (External) Assessment Board has been scheduled from **16th to**
uary 2022 from 10:30 AM at National Informatics Centre, A-Block, CGO Complex, Lodi R
Delhi – 110 003.

You are requested to kindly make it convenient to attend the meeting as per the sch
ned above.

(T.M. K
Joint Director

No.11017/92/2021-Coord./e-off:21441
भारत सरकार/Government of India
जल शक्ति मंत्रालय/Ministry of Jal Shakti
पेयजल एवं स्वच्छता विभाग/Deptt. Of Drinking Water and Sanitation
(समन्वय अनुभाग)/ (Coordination Section)

छठा तल, पंडित दीनदयाल अंत्योदय भवन,
सीजीओ कॉम्प्लेक्स, लोधी रोड
नई दिल्ली- 110003
दिनांक:31/08/2021

कार्यालय ज्ञापन

Subject: Identification of Key Performance Indicators (KPIs) for 40 blocks identified by DONER.

The undersigned is directed to refer to DO No. NEC-17/31/2021-O/o US (NEC) dated 4th August 2021 from Secretary, MoDNER on the subject mentioned above and to enclose herewith requisite information in respect of this Department.

2. Further, as desired, the details of Nodal Officer are as under:

i)	Name of Nodal officer	Shri Hiranya Borah
ii)	Designation:	Deputy Director General
iii)	Official E-Mail	hiranya.borah@nic.in
iv)	Mobile No.	9811890279
v)	Office Address	6th Floor, Pt. Deendayal Antyodaya Bhawan, CGO Complex Lodhi Road, New Delhi – 110003.
vi)	Landline No.	011-24369832

3. This issues with the approval of the competent authority.

Encl: As above.

(ओम प्रकाश)
अवर सचिव, भारत सरकार
दूरभाष नंबर 2436 1062

To

The Secretary,
Ministry of Development of North Eastern Region,
Vigyan Bhawan Annexe, Maulana Azad Road, New Delhi - 110011
Email ID: secydoner@nic.in

Copy to: DDG, DDWS – Alongwith a copy of ibid DO letter No. NEC-17/31/2021-O/o US (NEC) dated 4th August 2021 from Secretary, MoDNER on the above subject.

-1-

No: S-13015/9/2021-IEC and SBM-IV-DDWS
Government of India
Department of Drinking Water and Sanitation
Swachh Bharat Mission - Grameen

6th Floor, Pt. Deendayal Antrodaya Bhawan,
CGO Complex, Lodhi Road,
New Delhi-110 003
Date 8th November, 2021

OFFICE ORDER

Subject: Proposal for engagement of Programme Management Consultancy to manage the Social Media platforms for dissemination of information and spreading awareness about various day-today activities/events/measures/services/programmes etc. of the Centrally Sponsored Scheme viz. Swatchh Bharat Mission (Grameen)-Phase-II under DDWS. Constitution of Consultancy Evaluation Committee (CEC) – regarding.

With the approval of the competent authority, a Consultancy Evaluation Committee (CEC) is hereby constituted for engagement of 4 social media consultants for management of all platforms of social media for SBM(G) - phase -II, through Programme Management Consultancy Firm for one year from the date of acceptance of the offer and is extendable by one year subject to its satisfactory performance.

2. The composition of Consultancy Evaluation Committee is as under: -

Chairman	-	Shri Hiranya Borah, DDG(Stat.)
Member – I	-	Shri O. P Aggarwal, Sr.TD, NIC
Member – II	-	Shri Rajeev Saxena, US (Finance)
Member – III	-	Shri Sujoy Majumdar, WASH Specialist
Member Secretary	-	Sh. Ashvin Verma (SO/IEC)/ Sh. Sanjay Prakash (ASO/IEC)
Permanent Attendees	-	Shri Gajendra Singh, Consultant & Ms. Tulika Jha, Consultant

3. The Consultancy Evaluation Committee (CEC) shall be responsible for the selection process i.e. evaluation of EoI, short listing of consultants, deciding TORs, finalization & issuance of RfP, evaluation of technical and financial proposals, negotiations and final selection of the consultants.

(Rajeev Jauhari)
Dy. Secy. (IEC/Parl.)
Email: rajeev.j@gov.in
I-Com :- 416

To
All concerned Officer, DDWS

Copy for information to:
Sr PPS to Secretary (DDWS)/ PS to AS(SBMG)

No: S-13015/9/2021-IEC and SBM-IV-DDWS
Government of India
Department of Drinking Water and Sanitation
Swachh Bharat Mission - Grameen

6th Floor, Pt. Deendayal Antrodaya Bhawan,
CGO Complex, Lodhi Road,
New Delhi-110 003
Date 8th November, 2021

OFFICE ORDER

Subject: Proposal for engagement of Programme Management Consultancy to manage the Social Media platforms for dissemination of information and spreading awareness about various day-today activities/events/measures/services/programmes etc. of the Centrally Sponsored Scheme viz. Swatchh Bharat Mission (Grameen)-Phase-II under DDWS. Constitution of Consultancy Evaluation Committee (CEC) – regarding.

With the approval of the competent authority, a Consultancy Evaluation Committee (CEC) is hereby constituted for engagement of 4 social media consultants for management of all platforms of social media for SBM(G) - phase -II, through Programme Management Consultancy Firm for one year from the date of acceptance of the offer and is extendable by one year subject to its satisfactory performance.

2. The composition of Consultancy Evaluation Committee is as under: -

Chairman	-	Shri Hiranya Borah, DDG(Stat.)
Member – I	-	Shri O. P Aggarwal, Sr.TD, NIC
Member – II	-	Shri Rajeev Saxena, US (Finance)
Member – III	-	Shri Sujoy Majumdar, WASH Specialist
Member Secretary	-	Sh. Ashvin Verma (SO/IEC)/ Sh. Sanjay Prakash (ASO/IEC)
Permanent Attendees	-	Shri Gajendra Singh, Consultant & Ms. Tulika Jha, Consultant

3. The Consultancy Evaluation Committee (CEC) shall be responsible for the selection process i.e. evaluation of EoI, short listing of consultants, deciding TORs, finalization & issuance of RfP, evaluation of technical and financial proposals, negotiations and final selection of the consultants.

(Rajeev Jauhari)
Dy. Secy. (IEC/Parl.)
Email: rajeev.j@gov.in
I-Com :- 416

To
All concerned Officer, DDWS

Copy for information to:
Sr PPS to Secretary (DDWS)/ PS to AS(SBMG)

S-16011/2/2014-O/o Dir (SBM)
Government of India
Ministry of Jal Shakti
Department of Drinking Water and Sanitation
Swachh Bharat Mission (Grameen)

4th Floor, Pt. Deendayal 'AntyodayaBhawan'
CGO Complex, Lodi Road,
New Delhi-110 003
Dated- 11.09.2019

Office Memorandum

Subject: Constitution of Jury Committee for the category of Childern for Swachh Bharat Awards 2019

With the approval of the Secretary, DDWS, Jury Committee for the category of Children for Swachh Bharat Awards is constituted with following composition:

1. Shri Hiranya Borah, DDG, DDWS - Chairperson
2. Shri Yugal Kishore Joshi, Director, DDWS Ministry of Jal Shakti- Member-I
3. Shri Kapil Chaudhary, Director, DDWS Ministry of Jal Shakti- Member-II
4. Shri Mahesh Takhur, Deputy Secretary, DDWS Ministry of Jal Shakti- Member-III
5. Shri Sujoy Mojumdar, WASH expert, UNICEF- Member-IV

Sanju Yadav 11/9/19
(Sanju Yadav)
Assistant Director-IEC

To:

1. Shri Hiranya Borah,DDG, DDWS - Chairperson
2. Shri Yugal Kishore Joshi, Director, DDWS Ministry of Jal Shakti- Member-I
3. Shri Kapil Chaudhary, Director, DDWS Ministry of Jal Shakti- Member-II
4. Shri Mahesh Thakur, Deputy Secretary, DDWS Ministry of Jal Shakti- Member-III
5. Shri Sujoy Mojumdar, WASH expert, UNICEF- Member-IV

Copy to:

5. Sr. PS to Secretary
6. PS to JS (GA)

S-16011/2/2014-O/o Dir (SBM)
Government of India
Ministry of Jal Shakti
Department of Drinking Water and Sanitation
Swachh Bharat Mission (Grameen)

4[th]Floor, Pt. Deendayal 'AntyodayaBhawan'
CGO Complex, Lodi Road,
New Delhi-110 003
Dated- 11.09.2019

Office Memorandum

Subject: Constitution of Jury Committee for the category of Childern for Swachh Bharat Awards 2019

With the approval of the Secretary, DDWS, Jury Committee for the category of Children for Swachh Bharat Awards is constituted with following composition:

1. Shri Hiranya Borah, DDG, DDWS - Chairperson
2. Shri Yugal Kishore Joshi, Director, DDWS Ministry of Jal Shakti- Member-I
3. Shri Kapil Chaudhary, Director, DDWS Ministry of Jal Shakti- Member-II
4. Shri Mahesh Takhur, Deputy Secretary, DDWS Ministry of Jal Shakti- Member-III
5. Shri Sujoy Mojumdar, WASH expert, UNICEF- Member-IV

Sd/- 11/9/19
(Sanju Yadav)
Assistant Director-IEC

To:

1. Shri Hiranya Borah,DDG, DDWS - Chairperson
2. Shri Yugal Kishore Joshi, Director, DDWS Ministry of Jal Shakti- Member-I
3. Shri Kapil Chaudhary, Director, DDWS Ministry of Jal Shakti- Member-II
4. Shri Mahesh Thakur, Deputy Secretary, DDWS Ministry of Jal Shakti- Member-III
5. Shri Sujoy Mojumdar, WASH expert, UNICEF- Member-IV

Copy to:

5. Sr. PS to Secretary
6. PS to JS (GA)

Government of India
Ministry of Jal Shakti
Department of Drinking Water and Sanitation
Swachh Bharat Mission (Gramin)

6th Floor, Pt. DeendayalAntyodaya Bhawan
CGO Complex, Lodhi Road
New Delhi -110 003
Dated the 21 September, 2021

OFFICE ORDER

Subject: Composition of Committee to evaluatethe awardees forNational Level Wall PaintingCampaign conducted from 15th August, 2021 to 15th October, 2021 by DDWS on ODF plus themes – regarding.

Department of Drinking Water and Sanitation (DDWS), Ministry of Jal Shakti had launched a **National Level Wall Painting Campaign** on ODF Plus themes in rural context.

2. Under the campaign, all the villages across Gram Panchayats countrywide are expected to ensure these Wall Paintings at important public places in the village, like Panchayat office, school, community complexes/halls, haat bazars etc. These wall paintings aim at creating mass awareness on ODF Plus, in general and details specific to each theme (ODF sustainability Components: BWM, GOBARdhan, PWM, GWM, FSM) among the community members.

3. It has been decided that **3 best performing States based on total number of wall paintings on each theme, from each zone (3 positions x 5 themes x 6 zones = Total 90 awardees), will be felicitated at the National Level with certificate and memento virtually by Hon'ble MoJS, on 19th November, 2021**

4. A Committee as per following composition is hereby constituted forevaluation of the best 3 performing states on each theme, from each zone: -

Chairman	:	Shri Hiranya Borah, DDG, DDWS
Member	:	Sh. Om Prakash Aggarwal, Sr.TD/NIC, DDWS
Member	:	Shri Jay Prakash Narayan, US/Estt., DDWS
Member Secretary	:	Sh. Ashvin, SO(SBM-IEC)/ Sh. Sanjay, ASO(SBM-IEC)
Permanent Attendee	:	Sh. Gajendra, Consultant/SBM-IEC
Permanent Attendee	:	Shri Ikshwaku Sharma, Consultant/SBM

(Rajeev Jauhari)
Deputy Secretary (IEC&CB)
Email: rajeev.j@nic.in

Copy to :
1. All Members of the Committee
2. PS to Addition Secretary, SBM
3. PSO to Secretary, DDWS – for information of Secretary please

W-11042/80/2019-Water-II
Government of India
Ministry of Jal Shakti
Department of Drinking Water & Sanitation
(Water-II Section)

8th Floor, Pt.Deendayal, Antyodaya Bhawan,
CGO Complex, Lodi Road,
New Delhi-110 003

Dated: [illegible] June, 2019

OFFICE MEMORANDUM

Subject : **Constitution of a Multi-Disciplinary Committee to look into development issues and Special needs of the Eastern Nagaland-reg**

The undersigned is directed to refer to your Office Order No. 9/8/2012-I dated 12 June, 2019 regarding nomination as member of the committee and to say that the following officer is nominated with details below :-

1. DEPUTY DIRECTOR GENERAL (Shri Hiranya Borah), D/o DWS Mobile: 9811890279, Email: hiranya.borah@nic.in

(Vikas Srivastava)
Under Secretary to the Government. of India

To,

Deputy Secretary (NE III),
(A. Radha Rani),
NE I Section,
Ministry of Home Affairs,
North Block, New Delhi

Copy to :

Deputy Director General (Shri Hiranya Borah), DoDWS - for information alongwith a copy of MHA(NE I Section) Office Order No. 9/8/2012-I dated 12 June, 2019 for information please.

Government of India
Ministry of Jal Shakti
Department of Drinking Water and Sanitation
Swachh Bharat Mission (Gramin)

6th Floor, Pt. DeendayalAntyodaya Bhawan,
CGO Complex, Lodhi Road,
New Delhi -110 003
Dated the 21 September, 2021

OFFICE ORDER

Subject: Composition of Committee to evaluatethe awardees forNational Level Wall PaintingCampaign conducted from 15th August, 2021 to 15th October, 2021 by DDWS on ODF plus themes – regarding.

Department of Drinking Water and Sanitation (DDWS), Ministry of Jal Shakti had launched a **National Level Wall Painting Campaign** on ODF Plus themes in rural context.

2. Under the campaign, all the villages across Gram Panchayats countrywide are expected to ensure these Wall Paintings at important public places in the village, like Panchayat office, school, community complexes/halls, haat bazars etc. These wall paintings aim at creating mass awareness on ODF Plus, in general and details specific to each theme (ODF sustainability Components: BWM, GOBARdhan, PWM, GWM, FSM) among the community members.

3. It has been decided that **3 best performing States based on total number of wall paintings on each theme, from each zone (3 positions x 5 themes x 6 zones = Total 90 awardees), will be felicitated at the National Level with certificate and memento virtually by Hon'ble MoJS, on 19th November, 2021**

4. A Committee as per following composition is hereby constituted forevaluation of the best 3 performing states on each theme, from each zone: -

Chairman	:	Shri Hiranya Borah, DDG, DDWS
Member	:	Sh. Om Prakash Aggarwal, Sr.TD/NIC, DDWS
Member	:	Shri Jay Prakash Narayan, US/Estt., DDWS
Member Secretary	:	Sh. Ashvin, SO(SBM-IEC)/ Sh. Sanjay, ASO(SBM-IEC)
Permanent Attendee	:	Sh. Gajendra, Consultant/SBM-IEC
Permanent Attendee	:	Shri Ikshwaku Sharma, Consultant/SBM

(Rajeev Jauhari)
Deputy Secretary (IEC&CB)
Email: rajeev.j@nic.in

Copy to :

1. All Members of the Committee
2. PS to Addition Secretary, SBM
3. PSO to Secretary, DDWS – for information of Secretary please

File No. S-13015/17/2021-SBM-DDWS
Government of India
Ministry of Jal Shakti
Department of Drinking Water and Sanitation
Swachh Bharat Mission (Gramin)

12th Floor, Pt. Deendayal Antyodaya Bhawan,
CGO Complex, Lodhi Road,
New Delhi - 110 003
Dated the 31st August, 2021

OFFICE ORDER

Subject: Composition of a Committee to evaluate the entries received during the National Film Competition on different themes of ODF+ - regarding

Department of Drinking Water and Sanitation (DDWS), Ministry of Jal Shakti launched a National Level Competition of short films of duration 1-5 minutes on ODF Plus themes in rural context. The last date of submission of films was 31st August, 2021.

2. The award for the best entries at the State/UTs and District level will be given by the respective Committee for which the expenditure will be borne out of State IEC funds.

3. All States'/UTs' have been requested to send three best films to DDWS for National Level Selection on each geographical terrain and ODF plus theme. DDWS will select the three best entries in each category and disburse award at the National level with a certificate and Cash on Swachh Bharat Diwas i.e. 2nd October, 2021. The expenditure on prize money at National level will be met from DDWS IEC funds.

National Award Cash value:

	Overall Best Films in respective geographical terrain (five)	Thematic Winners (Six)
First prize:	5 x 2,00,000 = 10,00,000/-	6 x 1,00,000 = 6,00,000/-
First runner up:	5 x 1,20,000 = 6,00,000/-	6 x 60,000 = 3,60,000/-
Second runner up	5 x 80,000 = 4,00,000/-	6 x 30,000 = 1,80,000/-
Total	20,00,000/-	11,40,000/-
Total:		=Rs. 31,40,000/-

4. The entries in the film competition have been invited in the following two categories: -

Category 1 (Thematic Category): Based on the six components of ODF Plus:

(i) Bio-degradable waste management (BWM),
(ii) GOBARdhan,
(iii) Plastic Waste Management (PWM),
(iv) Greywater management (GWM),
(v) Faecal Sludge management (FSM), and
(vi) Behaviour Change.

F.No. S-13015/131/2019-SBM
Government of India
Ministry of Jal Shakti
Department of Drinking Water & Sanitation
Information, Education & Communication (IEC) Section

4th Floor, Pt. Deendayal Antyodaya Bhavan
CGO Complex, Lodhi Road,
New Delhi-110 003, the 30th June 2020

OFFICE ORDER

As approved by the Secretary, DDWS the following committee for selection of best District, Blocks, Panchayats/Village on the basis of total number of Community toilets constructed/painted during the Swachh Sundar Samudayik Shauchalaya campaign from 01st November 2019 to 30th April 2020, out of the nominations received from 12 states:-

1. Shri Hiranya Borah, DDG	Chairman
2. Smt Anupama, Director (SBM)	Member
3. Shri Mahesh Thakur, DS (SBM)	Member Secretary
4. Ms. Shalin Prasad, Communication for Development Specialist (UNICEF)	Member

The criteria for the States award -

- Number of CSCs constructed and geotagged (data from MIS) – 50%
- Number of CSCs constructed and geotagged in majority SC/ST populated villages (data from MIS) – 30%
- Quality of CSCs constructed (sample images from MIS) – 20%

The criteria for the district, block, and village award -

- Should be nominated by the State
- Quality of the community toilet, innovative O&M techniques, innovative IEC techniques

For more details, the committee may refer SSSS guidelines

The recommendations of the committee may be submitted to the Secretary, DWS within 10 days from the date of issue of this order.

30-6-2020
(Yugal Kishore Joshi)
Director (IEC)

To

The Chairman and all Members of the committee

Copy for information to:

1. PPS to Secretary, DWS
2. PS to AS (SBM) – for kind information of AS (SBM)
3. PS to JS (IEC) – for kind information of JS (IEC)
4. Ms. Shalini Prasad, Communication for Development Specialist (UNICEF)

An unparalleled "Generofficer"

Generosity is something which is expected from all. People expect to be treated generously not even from people in their personal life but also in professional front. They expect their bosses to be compassionate and generous as it enables them to work without succumbing to any kind of pressure and deliver the work with utmost sincerity and dedication. A generous boss gives his time, listens to you, doesn't demean you, instead encourages you so that you give your best to your organization. There are bosses out there who have a high degree of generosity instilled in them that their sub-ordinates feel fortunate to have them as their bosses and others wish to work with them. They can even make Mondays a joy. One such officer from our service (ISS) is **Shri Hiranya Borah Sir**. The persona he has can never be expressed in words.

Born to a teacher's family in a small village in Assam, Hiranya Borah Sir graduated from Cotton College, Guwahati in 1981 and finished his Masters & M.Phil from Delhi University. He worked as a lecturer in Cotton College for a few months in 1985 before joining the Government of India in the same year as an Indian Statistical Service (ISS) officer. He is inclined towards writing and started writing at a very young age. During his time at the College, he was the editor of the college magazine 'Cottonian'(1980) and had published two Assamese novels. Despite his busy schedule working for the GoI at a senior level post, he does not disappoint his readers and manages to write numerous books which are greatly appreciated and delight readers of all ages. He is now a successful author of more than 182 ebooks and has published 10 English books in print. Waiting for many more to come!

Apart from writing books, he is also a motivational speaker for the youngsters. I still remember, he had taken a session during our probation period and we were awestruck with his personality and the oratory skills he possesses.

He has always been praised for his great works. The greatest book he has ever written is 'Chandraprabha: The Iron Lady of Assam' which is an analytical biography of Padma Shri Chandraprabha Saikiani (1901-1972), who was a leading freedom fighter, social reformer, educationist and a pioneer of women empowerment of Assam. Luckily, I got this book for free from Sir. I read it and my mother too. Both of us enjoyed reading it! Great Work Sir!

The last time I met him was over a year ago. I was running late for work. Sir offered me a lift even though he was supposed to go in the opposite direction. I told Sir not to worry about me. But he said "Beta, I'll drop you to your office". He dropped me safely and on time just like a father would do for his daughter. Sir, I regret not working with you, however, I feel fortunate that I am one of those who you call Beta.

He was a lecturer, has successfully completed his Service in the Central Government and is a successful writer. He is a dedicated family man, Boss's favourite, a friend to his colleagues and a father like figure to his juniors. He's a thorough gentleman. Our Hon'ble Prime Minister Narendra Modi ji also tweeted about his book and shared a picture with him. That was a splendid click! You're so inspiring Sir!

Was delighted to receive a copy of the book 'Chandraprabha- The Iron Lady of Assam' penned by Shri Hiranya Borah. The book chronicles the life of the great Chandraprabha Saikiani, who made noteworthy contributions towards Assam's progress, social reform and empowerment of women.

4:32 pm · 16 Mar 21 · Twitter for iPhone

Sir, you write so much for your well-wishers. I am just offering a small tribute to you through this article, which is only a fraction of what you write for your readers. There are no words that can completely describe an awe-inspiring masterpiece like you and also your innumerable achievements. You are an inspiration for generations to come.

I would really like to express my deepest gratitude for all the kindness and generosity you have shown to us. Thanks a lot Sir. You are truly an unparalleled "Generofficer" of our Service! We always look up to you! Keep blessing us!

Wishing you a very Happy Retirement Sir!

Your Junior ISS officer,

DD(AK)

An article written by a junior officer, Kiruthika on me

Annexure-III

Highs and Lows of My Service Life and Beyond

Highs:

1. Meeting the Honourable PM Sir as a writer in his PMO office located inside the Parliament House is the highest point of my life.
2. Appointment as an Expert in the NCMS (National Court Management System) by the Honourable Chief Justice of India was another high point of my life.
3. Opening one RO office at Kohima, Nagaland and one SRO office at Imphal, Manipur of NSSO are two achievements of my life..
4. Appointment of Chairman of different committees of DDWS and MOSPI showed my worthiness as an officer.
5. Drafting of the first MDG Report for India and making of the first draft of coding for Time Use Survey of India under the High Level Seal Committee of Government of India give an idea about my technical capabilities.

6. Representing India in many International Forum as a Gender Specialist showed my depth of knowledge as an expert.

7. Purchasing of Office accommodations for RO, Assam and Zonal Office of NE, NSSO at Guwahati and SRO, Dibrugarh from Government Organisation was the testimony of my negotiating power.

8. Conducting of a Nation-wide survey on BSLLD (Basic Statistics on Local Level Development) in more than 100 districts covering all the states and UTs comprising more than 1 Lakh villages showed my endurance.

9. Looking after entire NE for making ODF by making at least 100 visits to these states wef January 2017 till all the states attained the ODF status much before the target date of 2nd October, 2019 had given an idea about my motivating capacity.

10. I was able to motivate few students/ youths in their career building

Lows:

1. I was awarded by a Delhi based senior officer average ACRS for consecutive 4 years when I was working in Assam as a Deputy Director. Except against the entry, Integrity, he

awarded me only a single word assessment 'Average' in all the entries of the ACR.

2. I was charge sheeted for a major punishment when I was initiating a file as a Director for allotting a contract to a firm under the instructions from my bosses details of the case have already given in the book.

3. I also got two recordable warnings while posting at Guwahati as a Regional Assistant Director and as a Deputy Director (My point of view has already been explained in details.)

4. Missed many promotions as a result of 'below benchmark' ACRS and being charge sheeted. From preliminary enquiry to the final settlement of the case lingered for almost ten years.

Silver lining of my life during this period:

1. All my children became financially settled with reasonably good salary.

2. I was posted in Nagaland (at that time insurgency problems in the state was at its peak) and Giridih where there was no basic facilities; but still I survived with dignity and pride.

3. Finally, I got the Vigilance clearance before my retirement and as a result of that I can

pursue my dream projects of making films and writing books on Lady Icons of India.

Regrets in Life:

Nothing except that I could not give sufficient time to my dying mother.

Satisfaction in life:

During my three years' tenure as Deputy Director, SSC, I was able to maintain utmost honesty and probably that is why, I need not have to tell anyone for employment of my children.

Coming from a background of a rural teachers' family, I was able to stay for more than 40 years (the last 20 years continuously) in Delhi with head high.

Only officer from my service who has written more than 200 ebooks and 14 printed published books.

A privileged person on whose mother's childhood a telefilm has been made by DD.

A privileged officer based on whose stories an Assamese telefilm and a Hindi serial have been made by DD so far.

Annexure-IV

List of published books and ebooks written by me:

List of published printed books

1. Random Thoughts through a Coloured Prism
2. Melody of Fragrance
3. Guilt: Gift of Winter Spring
4. How to become unpopular
5. Twenty-five Love Stories
6. Aparajita: Short Stories
7. Random Stories and Dilemma of an old man
8. Father's Choice: A Story of True Love
9. Three Goddesses and only one Rascal
10. Blessed One

11. Chandraprabha: The Iron Lady of Assam

11. Mula Gabharu: A Story of Extreme Valour and Patriotism

12. Blessed One: Part-II

13. Seuz Jonack (Assamese)

14. Meghar Arar Surya (Assamese)

List of ebooks:

1. Random Thoughts

2. Dilemma of a Young Mind

3. Funny Statistics and Serious Statisticians

4. Melody of Fragrance

5. Akhadya

6. Few Cities through the Lens of Hiranya Borah

7. Guilt: Gift of Winter Spring

8.Beautiful Ghost

9. Great Fighters: Grace of God

10. All Blurred

11. Putting kids to sleep

12. How to become unpopular

13. Soulmates

14. My grumpy Face

95. An Unusual Love Affair

96. Birth Day

97. Do not Tell Anyone

98. Anupama

99. Late By Ten Years

100. Murder in a Foreign City

101. Strange Life

102. I love You Darling

103. Falsehood

104. Lady in the Park

105. Do Anything, I Shall comment

106. Professionalism

107. Art of Flirting

108. Are We Human

109. Old man and a Dog

110. Relation with Relatives

111. Sun and Cloud

112. My Second Lover

113. In a Meeting

114. Love at First Sight

115. A Psalm of Life

116. He Wants a Solution

117. Wings

118. Twenty-five Love Stories

119. Me and a Dozen Plus One Ghost Stories

120. AparAjita: Twenty Seven Short Stories

121. Nothing Official As Such

122. Illustrated Kids' Story

123. Hundred Ways to F & F your Popularity

124. Broken heart

125. Random Stories and Dilemma

126. A Phone Call

127. Revenge

128. Men, Women, Dogs and Bitches

129. Mera Pyar (Hindi)

130. Scandal

131. Anuradha

132. Looking for a wife at thirteen

133. Fenny My Hero

134. Frustration: How to Get Rid of It

175. Chandra Prabha Saikiani

176. Beautiful Promises of the First Night

177. In the Highest Court of Justice (Drama)

178. My Teachers

179. An Incomplete Voyage of a Blessed One

180. Nothing Personal

181. Covid 19 Vs 2020 Wonderful Warriors

182. Communication skill

183. Covid Test

184. Sati Sadhani: The tragedy Queen of Assam

185. Subhra Shatadal: The Stunning Beauty

186. Mula Gabharu: The Ultimate Woman Warrior of Assam

187. Shoes with Wings

Connect with him

Email: hbmb@rediffmail.com

Friend him on Facebook: hbmb@rediffmail.com

For Tweeter: hbmb@rediffmail.com

Website: Hiranya.com

Website: Hiranyaboraauthor.com

9 789356 113992

Printed by Libri Plureos GmbH in Hamburg,
Germany